The Daily Telegraph
Improve Your Bridge at Home

Tony Forrester

B. T. Batsford Ltd, *London*

First published 1995

© Tony Forrester 1995

ISBN 0 7134 7779 2

A CIP catalogue record for this book is available from the British Library.

Typeset by Apsbridge Services Ltd, Nottingham.
Printed by Redwood Books, Trowbridge, Wiltshire
for the publishers,
B. T. Batsford Ltd, 4 Fitzhardinge Street,
London W1H 0AH

A BATSFORD BRIDGE BOOK
Series Editor: Tony Sowter

CONTENTS

INTRODUCTION   5

PART ONE   DECLARER PLAY

Chapter One   PLAYING TRUMP CONTRACTS   7

                When to Choose a Trump Contract
                The Use of Trumps
                When to Draw Trumps
                Effective Techniques with Trumps

Chapter Two   PLAYING NO TRUMP CONTRACTS   37

                Introduction and Objectives
                Establishing Tricks
                More Advanced Techniques

PART TWO   DEFENCE

Chapter Three   OPENING LEADS   61

                Introduction
                Which Suit do we Lead?
                Which Card do we Lead?
                Switching the Defence

Chapter Four   GENERAL PRINCIPLES OF
                DEFENSIVE PLAY   81

                Third Hand High
                Finessing Against Dummy
                Second Hand Low
                Covering an Honour

Chapter Five   SIGNALS AND DISCARDS   99

        Signals
        Discards

PART THREE   BIDDING

Chapter Six   HIGH-LEVEL OPENINGS
        AND RESPONSES   109

        The Two Level
        The Three Level
        Responding to Three-Level Openings
        The Four Level

Chapter Seven RANGE OF 1NT AND 2NT OPENINGS
        AND REBIDS   121

Chapter Eight   JUMP RESPONSES   125

        CONCLUSION   128

INTRODUCTION

This book is designed to build on the knowledge gained in *Play Bridge at Home*, but I hope to make it more than just 'the second in a series'. I want all home bridge enthusiasts, whether they have just begun the game, or have been playing for many years, to use it to develop their skills.

I will look at all aspects of the game – declarer play, defence and bidding – and expand on many of the themes that I started in the first book. Most of all, I wish to entertain you, because any text, however well intentioned, will fail to keep its audience if it lacks lighter moments.

Without labouring points, I intend to err on the side of going slowly rather than rushing along, so bear with me if you think I am dawdling over some areas. I firmly believe that a book which sets out to increase the knowledge of its readers must take care not to assume too much, nor to show-off the writer's abilities. I hope you will feel that I have avoided both these pitfalls.

Tony Forrester
1995

1
PLAYING TRUMP CONTRACTS

When to Choose a Trump Contract

There are two fundamental decisions made in any sequence, how high to play and whether to select 'trumps' or 'no trumps'. To be consistently successful in those decisions requires an understanding of the role of trumps in declarer play. That, in turn, enables us to judge the trick-taking potential of a hand, and assists us in choosing a sensible contract.

Before we tackle some of the most important aspects of playing a suit contract, let me first outline some of the key factors which should determine when and how we select a trump suit.

It is always absolutely essential to have as many cards in our trump suit as possible, regardless of their strength. We should prefer length to strength. Consider these two hands:

♠ AKJ
♡ 9543
◇ QJ4
♣ A73

```
  N
W   E
  S
```

♠ Q1094
♡ J10872
◇ AK5
♣ 6

North/South have to pick a final contract. Should they select spades where they hold all the top six cards, or hearts, where they have greater length? The answer lies in how we use trumps. Here, repeated club leads by the defenders will force South to ruff (to prevent East/West winning easy tricks). If that ruff materially weakens the trump suit, the danger signs start flashing.

If North/South finish in spades, because of the greater strength there, South's first ruff will reduce South's trump holding to three cards, and leave open the door for any defender holding four or more spades to gain the upper hand. I can assure you that there are few things more annoying than the defenders using *their* trumps on your winners.

This should not happen if hearts is the chosen trump suit. True, there are more top trump 'losers' as such, *but* these tricks will have to be lost in any case, regardless of the contract. There can be no escaping the loss of at least two heart tricks. The gain is that declarer's need to ruff clubs does not reduce South's number of trumps below the level of his opponents'.

As North/South have nine hearts between them, the strong likelihood is that neither East nor West hold more than three cards in the suit. Hence, South can safely ruff a couple of times without jeopardising 'trump control'. I will return to this theme shortly.

Having established that the first priority is to choose the combined longest suit, is there a minimum number of trumps that we should feel comfortable with? I would suggest you stick with eight card fits for now, when you have a choice.

For example:

♠ Q4
♡ KJ95
◇ AQ632
♣ J9

N
W E
S

♠ AJ732
♡ Q7
◇ K4
♣ K1073

With 26 points between them, North/South have the requirements for a game contract. Let us see how the bidding might develop – with South dealer.

West	North	East	South
–	–	–	1♠
Pass	2◊	Pass	2♠
Pass	3♡	Pass	3NT
Pass	Pass	Pass	

South rebids spades over North's 2◊ response, guaranteeing at least five cards in the suit. North could simply bid 4♠, knowing that they have at least a seven card fit and the high card requirements for 4♠. Instead, North bids 3♡ and quite right too.

To begin with, this bid describes the hand further and it gives South a chance to put the finishing touches to 'painting' a picture of the hand. With only five indifferent spades and good clubs, no trumps is the obvious choice. However, let me make a small change to the South hand:

♠ Q4
♡ KJ95
◊ AQ632
♣ J9

♠ AJ10873
♡ A62
◊ K7
♣ 43

West	North	East	South
–	–	–	1♠
Pass	2◊	Pass	2♠
Pass	3♡	Pass	3♠
Pass	4♠	Pass	Pass
Pass			

Here North's bidding has enabled the partnership to reach 4♠, rather than 3NT. Did they do the right thing?

Well, now they have that crucial eighth trump I was talking about earlier, which will allow South to handle the suit easily, even if the opposing spades divide badly (e.g. four in one hand and one in the other, or 4-1).

Further, neither North nor South has any protection in clubs, and cannot prevent their opponents winning many tricks in the suit in no trumps. As East/West have nine clubs between them, it is certain that one player holds at least five and hence they will be able to defeat 3NT by simply cashing the suit.

North's careful and descriptive bidding has steered his side into the correct game contract on two completely separate occasions. We have also seen two of the basic *rules for selection of a trump suit:*

1. Possession of eight or more cards in the suit.
2. The absence of a stop in a given suit.

Is one of these rules more important than the other? Look at these two hands, and you will see the answer:

♠ Q4
♡ KJ95
◇ AQ632
♣ J9

♠ AKJ93
♡ Q73
◇ K4
♣ 432

North/South have a problem. Two good hands, but no eight-card fit anywhere to be seen, and no stop in clubs. According to what I have said so far, they cannot play this hand at all! Let us look at the bidding and how it might resolve the problem.

West	North	East	South
–	–	–	1♠
Pass	2◇	Pass	2♠
Pass	3♡	Pass	4◇(i)
Pass	4♠(ii)	Pass	Pass(iii)
Pass			

(i) South has nowhere obvious to go. He cannot sensibly repeat his spades because he has already shown all the five he has, and another spade bid would guarantee at least six. He cannot reasonably bid 3NT because although he holds three cards in the 'unbid' suit, clubs, he cannot have three more useless ones! By definition, he cannot 'stop' the opponents running the suit, all he can do is watch. Hence, he shows 'delayed' diamond support, suggesting that, if pushed into a corner, he has tolerance for diamonds but that he would not volunteer it. He is waiting to see what develops.

(ii) North fears that South has only limited interest in diamonds, so he is afraid to commit to an 11 trick game. Hence, he tries 4♠ implying that he too has mild support, but nothing to get excited about. He is offering South a 'choice of contracts' between 4♠ and 5◊.

(iii) South is delighted to stay in spades for two reasons:

(a) His suit is excellent, given the fact that he has already denied holding six cards.
(b) To make game in spades requires one trick less than in diamonds.

So we have found that the absence of a 'stop' in a given suit makes a trump contract desirable, regardless of whether there is an eight card fit or not. In other words *Rule 2 overrides Rule 1*. Are there times when life is not so comfortable? Look at this example:

♠ J7
♡ K1073
◊ Q6
♣ J9532

```
      N
   W     E
      S
```

♠ AQ654
♡ Q6
◊ AJ942
♣ 4

West	North	East	South
–	–	–	1♠
Pass	1NT	Pass	2◊
Pass	2♠	Pass	Pass
Pass			

When a partnership has more limited resources, i.e. not sufficient to reach game, they do not have the luxury of 'time' and 'space'. The bidding will usually be brief, because a longer sequence would necessitate playing at a higher level than they can aspire to. Frequently this leads to a second-best contract being selected (or sometimes even worse than that).

In this particular example, North is faced with only two realistic options: pass 2♢ or bid 2♠. Neither contract looks particularly appetising: in fact, a return to 1NT would be preferable. Nevertheless, as an obedient partner, North chooses between spades and diamonds. The objective is simple: to pick the suit with the most trumps. As South starts the bidding with the longest suit, 2♠ cannot realistically be worse than 2♢, and may well be better.

Despite both players bidding immaculately, they have arrived in a dubious contract which is a trump short of our desired minimum. Sadly, this occurs much more frequently than we would wish it to. Hence, it is important to know how to handle all kinds of trump contracts, from the big fits where we have ten or eleven cards in a suit, down to the rickety-gate ones with only seven.

It is time to move on to some of the techniques that we use, but, first of all, a brief re-cap of this part with a little quiz:

Quiz

1. Which key factors determine whether to play a trump contract?
2. Which is the most important of these?
3. How should you select the trump suit?
4. What is the optimum contract for these pairs of hands:

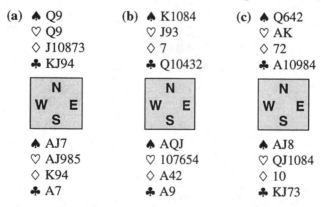

(a)	♠ Q9	(b)	♠ K1084	(c)	♠ Q642
	♡ Q9		♡ J93		♡ AK
	♢ J10873		♢ 7		♢ 72
	♣ KJ94		♣ Q10432		♣ A10984
	♠ AJ7		♠ AQJ		♠ AJ8
	♡ AJ985		♡ 107654		♡ QJ1084
	♢ K94		♢ A42		♢ 10
	♣ A7		♣ A9		♣ KJ73

5. How do you think the hands should be bid (South is always the dealer)?

Answers

1. (a) You have a combined holding of at least 8 cards in a given suit
(b) You cannot 'stop' or 'guard' a suit.

2. (b) is more important

3. The suit with the highest number of cards in it. If you have two 'equal' suits, the higher ranking one is normally best (because it scores more when it makes!)

4.   (a) 3NT   **(b)** 2♡   **(c)** 5♣

5.

(a)

West	North	East	South
–	–	–	1♡
Pass	1NT	Pass	2NT
Pass	3NT	Pass	Pass
Pass			

(b)

West	North	East	South
–	–	–	1♡
Pass	1♠	Pass	1NT
Pass	2♡(i)	Pass	Pass
Pass			

(i)   Not 2♣, which would tend to show a better hand.

(c)

West	North	East	South
–	–	–	1♡
Pass	2♣	Pass	3♣
Pass	3♠(i)	Pass	5♣
Pass	Pass	Pass	

(i)   Avoid gambling on 3NT, when you can make a descriptive bid and let partner decide.

Don't be surprised if your sequences do not match mine. I would not expect them to. The beauty of bridge is in its subjectivity and nothing is more subjective than a view of what a player should bid. Agreeing on a bidding sequence with another expert is as rare for me as agreeing with Terry Venables' choice of England team! We all have a view and we are all right – that's one of the factors that makes bridge stimulating.

The Use of Trumps

We already know that a trump is more powerful than an ace in some circumstances. It is crucial to our development as bridge players that we harness that power properly. This part will deal, in a general way, with some of the common uses of trumps, before I move on, in my third book, to more advanced techniques.

Let me begin with an exercise in hand evaluation. Your partner opens 1♠: how do you respond with the following hands?

(a)   ♠ A932   (b)   ♠ A932   (c)   ♠ A9753
      ♡ K75   ♡ K75   ♡ K75
      ◊ J94   ◊ J9632   ◊ J9632
      ♣ 632   ♣ 4   ♣ –

I hope you selected (a) 2♠, (b) 3♠ and (c) 4♠. Why should you make three different bids, even though you had exactly the same number of points? The answer lies in the distribution of the hands and awareness that a singleton (or ideally a void), *allied to strong trump support*, represents power. To see why, let us place those hands opposite an unspectacular minimum opening bid, and examine how our bidding worked out:

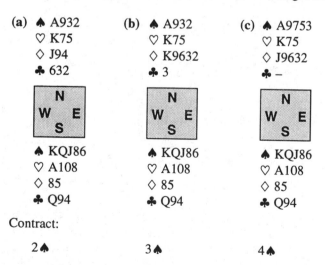

(a)   ♠ A932   (b)   ♠ A932   (c)   ♠ A9753
      ♡ K75   ♡ K75   ♡ K75
      ◊ J94   ◊ K9632   ◊ J9632
      ♣ 632   ♣ 3   ♣ –

      ♠ KQJ86   ♠ KQJ86   ♠ KQJ86
      ♡ A108   ♡ A108   ♡ A108
      ◊ 85   ◊ 85   ◊ 85
      ♣ Q94   ♣ Q94   ♣ Q94

Contract:

   2♠   3♠   4♠

In hand (a) we will have our work cut out to even make 2♠. We would analyse our prospects as follows:

Spades	–	No losers
Hearts	–	1 loser
Diamonds	–	2 losers
Clubs	–	3 losers (or 2 if East has ♣AK)

Note how we look at a trump or suit contract in a different way to no trumps. There, we examine our quick tricks first, and if a deficiency exists, we 'establish' the balance. Suit playing is more geared to 'losers', although the analysis can provide similar results. In (a) for instance, we could equally have said:

Spades	=	5 quick tricks
Hearts	=	2 quick tricks
Diamonds	=	0
Clubs	=	0
Total		**7**

We are one short, so next we assess our 'establishable' tricks:

Spades	=	0
Hearts	=	0
Diamonds	=	0
Clubs	=	$^1/_4$ (When ♣AK are both with East)
Total	=	$^1/_4$

It didn't take us long to add that up! We are one trick short in all probability and will suffer defeat.

How did our decision to raise partner to 3♠ with hand (b) get along?

(b)

> ♠ A932
> ♡ K75
> ◇ J9632
> ♣ 3

```
        N
    W       E
        S
```

> ♠ KQJ86
> ♡ A108
> ◇ 85
> ♣ Q94

Our losers are as follows:

Spades	=	0
Hearts	=	1
Diamonds	=	2
Clubs	=	1
Total	=	**4**

With only four losers, it is reasonable to assume that our nine-trick contract will be successful. Hand (b) appears on the surface to be almost two tricks better than (a). Why is this?

The reason lies in its distribution, in particular the singleton club. Because we are intending to play in a suit contract, a singleton becomes a very powerful feature in a hand. Here, South can ruff clubs in the North hand after letting the opponents win only one trick in the suit. The fact that South may have three losing clubs will not matter, they can simply be led in order to use dummy's trumps. In this way, we are creating and making a strength out of a weakness.

In passing, let us look briefly at how our analysis based on tricks would work out here. First, quick tricks would be seven, as before, and establishable tricks would be one (for diamonds), giving us a total of eight. If we played the hand as if we were in no trumps, we would be defeated. We must make good use of our trumps to avoid that.

(c)

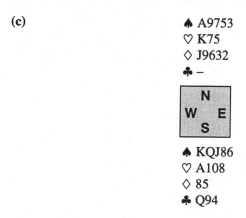

♠ A9753
♡ K75
◇ J9632
♣ –

♠ KQJ86
♡ A108
◇ 85
♣ Q94

In (c) we raised to game despite having only eight points. How do we justify this?

It is sensible to have a rule of thumb for *evaluating the effects of distribution* and I would recommend the following:

1.   With four card trump support *add*:

> 1 point if holding a doubleton
> 2 points if holding a singleton
> 3 points if holding a void

2.   With five card trump support *add*:

> 1 point if holding a doubleton
> 3 points if holding a singleton
> 4 points if holding a void

With three card trump support, I would add one point with a doubleton, and two points with a singleton or void.

On that basis, our North hand (c) is worth 12 points (8 high card points, plus 4 for the void allied to five spades) or a minimum opening bid, thoroughly justifying the apparently wild leap to game. North is exonerated for now!

When to Draw Trumps

How do we translate this apparent strength of North's hand into tricks? It is time to work at declarer play and let me start with this as my first example.

West leads ♣A after our sequence of 1♠-4♠, how do we proceed? Think about it for a moment before reading on.

We start by ruffing the opening lead and our next key decision is the most important and fundamental to successful suit play.

'Do we Draw Trumps or Not?'

There are far too many variations in play to be dogmatic here and a generalisation would do more harm than good. However, there are one or two situations which demand a certain treatment and I will endeavour to cover those shortly. For now, I suggest that you always ask yourself certain questions before deciding how to proceed in any suit contract:

1. If I draw trumps, will I have enough top tricks left to make the contract?

2. If I draw trumps, and I do not have enough top tricks, will I have enough trumps to ruff out my 'losers'? Or, failing that, can I establish sufficient tricks for my contract?

As long as you can answer 'yes' to any of the questions, you should draw trumps. This is by no means a perfect solution to all hands and as you gain in expertise you will start to see the exceptions for yourself, but it will do for the time being. Here is an illustration:

Dealer South. Love All.

> ♠ J432
> ♡ J98
> ◊ A7
> ♣ Q1098

	N	
W		E
	S	

> ♠ AKQ108
> ♡ 107
> ◊ 63
> ♣ AKJ7

West	North	East	South
–	–	–	1♠
Pass	2♠	Pass	4♠
Pass	Pass	Pass	

West leads ♡ A and follows with the king and a third round to East's queen which you ruff. Ask yourself the key questions to determine if you should draw trumps. In fact, the first answer provides us with all we require because we can see enough top tricks:

Spades	=	5
Diamonds	=	1
Clubs	=	4
		10

Hence you draw the opposing trumps immediately and cash your winners.

♠ A9753
♡ K75
◇ J9632
♣ –

♠ KQJ86
♡ A108
◇ 85
♣ Q94

Back, yet again, to hand (c). Do we draw trumps or not? Question 2 is apposite here, because we have to ruff out the two remaining club losers in the South hand, to achieve our Contract. If we draw the opposing trumps, will we succeed?

The answer is that we should, because the opponents have only three spades between them and the normal division is 2-1. Consequently, two rounds of the suit should suffice. North's five spades will be used as follows:

> 2 for drawing the opponents trumps
> 3 for ruffing South's clubs.

If one opponent shows out on the first round of spades, we will have to consider a change of strategy and we will move on to that after a short break:

Quiz

1. If partner opens 1♡, what would you bid the following hands?

<table>
<tr><td>(a)</td><td>♠ AQ4</td><td>(b)</td><td>♠ 4</td><td>(c)</td><td>♠ 74</td></tr>
<tr><td></td><td>♡ J984</td><td></td><td>♡ A10842</td><td></td><td>♡ QJ73</td></tr>
<tr><td></td><td>◇ K107</td><td></td><td>◇ A10732</td><td></td><td>◇ QJ4</td></tr>
<tr><td></td><td>♣ J93</td><td></td><td>♣ J6</td><td></td><td>♣ K1093</td></tr>
</table>

2. Is the following statement True or False –

'In a no trump contract, one counts tricks, but in a suit contract one should normally count losers'?

3. What is the fundamental decision to make when playing a suit contract?

Answers

1. (a) 3♡   **(b)** 4♡   **(c)** 3♡ (Just. Close between
                                                             2♡ & 3♡)

2. True

3. Whether to draw trumps.

Effective Techniques with Trumps

Ruffs in Dummy

Let us return to our 4♠ contract, for the last time I assure you, and see all four hands (something only allowed in books, I am afraid):

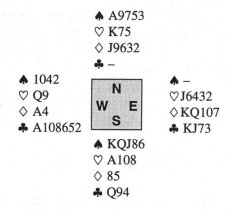

```
                    ♠ A9753
                    ♡ K75
                    ◇ J9632
                    ♣ –
    ♠ 1042                         ♠ –
    ♡ Q9           N              ♡ J6432
    ◇ A4        W     E           ◇ KQ107
    ♣ A108652      S              ♣ KJ73
                    ♠ KQJ86
                    ♡ A108
                    ◇ 85
                    ♣ Q94
```

We ruffed West's opening lead of ♣A and continued with a trump to the jack, proposing to draw the remaining trump if both East and West follow suit. Sadly, East does not. We must now change horses and consider how to develop the hand without drawing trumps immediately.

In summary, *we must leave trumps alone* when any of these statements holds true:

1. We need to produce extra tricks and we do not have a suit to establish.
2. We will remove all our trumps without enough quick tricks to ensure the contract.
3. We may lose 'trump control' (I will discuss this term in more depth later).

Here we fall into category (1), i.e. we do not have enough tricks if we draw *three* rounds of trumps. Hence, we must proceed as follows: at trick three, we play another club and ruff in dummy, then we play a heart to South's ace and yet another club (our last) again ruffed in dummy.

With all our clubs safely out of the way, there is no further role for dummy's one remaining trump to perform. We can now continue with the process of drawing the enemy trumps. At the end of the hand, we will have made:

5   Spade tricks
3   Ruffs in dummy (of declarer's clubs)
2   Heart tricks (ace and king)

We have managed our contract with only 20 points (or an exactly equal share) via excellent use of trumps – providing us with eight of the ten tricks. An adequate demonstration of the power of great combined length in a suit *allied* to shortages, i.e. singleton or voids.

All experts would say 'Give me distribution in preference to points'. After all there is something rather nice about your little trump being more powerful than the opponents' ace. As you have just seen, it is quite possible for an 8 point hand to be 'worth' more than an 11 point one, simply because of the distribution it possesses.

How would you tackle the play of this hand?

Dealer South. Love All.

```
            ♠ 7
            ♡ A987
            ◊ J8432
            ♣ AJ5
          ┌─────────┐
          │    N    │
          │  W   E  │
          │    S    │
          └─────────┘
            ♠ A94
            ♡ KQJ62
            ◊ 76
            ♣ Q108
```

West	North	East	South
–	–	–	1♡
Pass	4♡	Pass	Pass
Pass			

A short sharp sequence to an eminently sensible contract, North realising that his apparently average hand of 10 points was, in fact, quite potent. West leads ♣2 and you have to plan the play. Decide for yourself, before reading on.

Let us begin by looking at our losers:

Spades	=	0
Hearts	=	0
Diamonds	=	2
Clubs	=	$^1/_2$ (if East has ♣K)
Total		**$2^1/_2$**

It appears, superficially, to be an extremely simple hand. However, it is at such times that we must be vigilant. Remember this rule and you will not go far wrong:

'When the contract appears simple, beware of bad breaks.'

This contract is surely safe? All we need to do is to play low in dummy and we will make an eleventh trick when West has ♣K, ten otherwise. Easy!

Beware of greed and complacency, because *until you have secured the lead* and drawn trumps there is always danger. Just look at this layout and you will see what I mean:

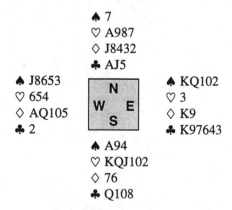

```
                  ♠ 7
                  ♡ A987
                  ◇ J8432
                  ♣ AJ5
    ♠ J8653        ┌─────────┐      ♠ KQ102
    ♡ 654         │    N    │       ♡ 3
    ◇ AQ105       │ W     E │       ◇ K9
    ♣ 2           │    S    │       ♣ K97643
                  └─────────┘
                  ♠ A94
                  ♡ KQJ102
                  ◇ 76
                  ♣ Q108
```

If a small club is played from dummy, East will win the king and return the suit for his partner to ruff. Now the ace and king of diamonds will be cashed and yet another club from East will be ruffed by West. You have lost the first five tricks. Two down. What is worse is that partner is scowling across the table at you and is about to explain where you went wrong. Can you interrupt him?

We should realise that we have a *safe* ten tricks and play accordingly. We rise with ♣A and play a spade to South's ace followed by a spade ruff in dummy. Now a trump to South's 10 and another ruff (this time with the ace of trumps to avoid 'blocking' the suit). Then we draw trumps and concede a club trick to whosoever has ♣K. We guarantee:

1	Spade trick
2	Spade ruffs in dummy
5	trump tricks in South
2	Club tricks
10	**Tricks in total**

However the East/West cards are divided we secure our contract. It is quite possible that an extra trick could have been achieved by playing a low club at trick one (i.e. West has ♣K), but we would have risked our contract and that risk is unacceptable. Play safely whenever you can.

The Cross-ruff
This phrase sounds like it should come from 'The Sting', but is in fact one of our most valuable techniques. So far we have concentrated on hands where we gained extra tricks by using dummy's trumps to ruff losers in declarer's hand. We can carry this principle further.

♠ 3
♡ QJ98
◊ A7543
♣ 987

♠ A842
♡ AK104
◊ 2
♣ J1064

Just to see the importance of ruffing, let us assume that you (or more likely, your partner!) have had something of a brainstorm, and bid to 4♡ despite holding only 19 combined points. West leads ◊Q, how can you extricate yourself from this mess?

If you draw the enemy trumps, you will have at most eight tricks (three trumps, two ruffs, ♠A, ◇A and maybe a club). The technique of ruffing spades in dummy whilst drawing trumps will also fall well short of the mark (four trumps, two ruffs, ◇A, ♠A).

You have to 'cross-ruff', *using trumps in* **both** *hands completely separately*. In this way, you aim to contrive eight trump tricks, ♠A and ◇A. You cannot afford any rounds of trumps at all.

So you win ◇A and ruff a diamond at trick two, then play ♠A and a spade ruff in dummy. You continue with this game of ping-pong, diamond ruffs in hand and spade ruffs in dummy, until there is nothing left to ruff with. The last three cards in each hand will be clubs, whilst the defence will have an array of trumps, aces, kings and queens. No matter, you have made your contract and you don't care what happens thereafter.

As an aside, it is important to note that a cross-ruff not only demands the ability to score ruffs in both hands, but also that your trumps are of good quality. It is important that the opposition will not be able to 'over-ruff' at any stage, as this will cause your plan to collapse. In this example, you are blessed with all the top hearts down to the eight, so your only danger, marginal as it is, is that ♡4 is over-ruffed by West. For this to happen he would have to possess a singleton diamond, and that is extremely unlikely.

Suit Establishment
The last technique involving the use of trumps, that I intend to cover for now, is that of *establishing a suit by ruffing*. Here is a typical example:

Dealer South. Game All.

♠ 74
♡ K752
◇ A8765
♣ K7

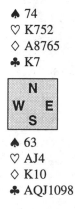

♠ 63
♡ AJ4
◇ K10
♣ AQJ1098

West	North	East	South
–	–	–	1♣
Pass	1◇	Pass	3♣
Pass	3♡	Pass	4♣
Pass	5♣	Pass	Pass
Pass			

You have arrived in an excellent contract of 5♣ (isn't bidding easy?) and, before we consider the play, just look over the hand yourself and decide how you would proceed. East/West begin by cashing two rounds of spades and then switch to a trump.

Generally, we create extra tricks by ruffing losers in the shorter trump hand, nearly always dummy. We do not gain tricks, as such, by ruffing with the longer trump suit, because long trumps would win tricks anyway.

However, we can use declarer's trumps to 'establish' suits in dummy. Having established these suits, we can then discard losers on them.

With that subtle hint about how we might play the contract, let us now look at our 5♣ contract. We have three distinct routes that we could follow:

1. Draw trumps and take the heart finesse.

2. Draw trumps, play ◇K and ◇A and lead a third diamond, ruffing in hand. If the East/West diamonds divide 3-3, we will have two winners in dummy on which to discard hearts. We no longer need the heart finesse. If the suit divides 4-2 (which is slightly more probable than 3-3) we revert to the heart finesse.

3. Win the trump switch in hand. Cash ◇K, ◇A and ruff a diamond (as in 2 above). Now, if the suit has divided 4-2, i.e. one player shows out on the third round, cross to ♣K to ruff a further diamond. Then draw trumps. We will have at least one diamond winner in dummy, on which to throw a heart.

Each line is an improvement on the previous one. In shorthand, we can summarise the chances as:

Line 1: ♡Q is with East or about 50% (1 in 2)
Line 2: ♡Q with East, or diamonds 3-3 about 67% (2 in 3)
Line 3: ♡Q with East or diamonds no worse than 4-2 about 90% (9 in 10)

Our failure rate has gone down from 1 in 2 to 1 in 10, by recognising the need to establish the diamonds in dummy, and then using the best technique to achieve that.

Quick Discards

Normally in bridge, the measured approach is best. There are occasions, though, when urgency is the name of the game. Look at this example and you will see what I mean:

Dealer East. Love All.

♠ 984
♡ A652
◇ K6
♣ K764

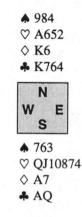

♠ 763
♡ QJ10874
◇ A7
♣ AQ

West	North	East	South
–	–	Pass	1♡
Pass	3♡	Pass	4♡
Pass	Pass	Pass	

West, for once, fails to make the best lead of a spade, and selects ◇ Q. It appears tempting to win with the ace and immediately finesse in trumps. If the finesse loses, however, East will surely find a spade switch (particularly if he or she reads Chapter 3 of this book!), and down you will go.

However, we do have ten tricks, even when the heart finesse fails (five hearts, two diamonds and three clubs) so surely we should take those tricks, and ignore the possible jibes of 'not being able to take a finesse' if ♡K proves to be with West.

Hence, we win ◇ A, play a trump to the ace (just in case the king is singleton and we can complete drawing trumps) and then cash ♣AQ. Next, we cross to dummy with ◇ K and play ♣K, discarding a losing spade. At worst, we should make ten tricks, occasionally we make eleven as here for example:

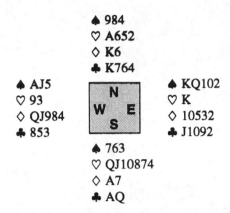

♠ 984
♡ A652
◇ K6
♣ K764

♠ AJ5
♡ 93
◇ QJ984
♣ 853

♠ KQ102
♡ K
◇ 10532
♣ J1092

♠ 763
♡ QJ10874
◇ A7
♣ AQ

When we are in *quick discard* mode, we must always be careful to leave our 'entries' in a satisfactory state. Entries are often the vital factor in making a contract, and their power can easily be seen by altering the North/South hands on the previous example:

♠ 984
♡ QJ102
◇ 63
♣ K764

♠ 763
♡ A87654
◇ AK
♣ AQ

Contract 4♡ by South.

West's lead of ◇ Q may escape unharmed if this was the layout. Although we have ten tricks, we probably cannot get at one of them, because the North hand has no quick entry. How frustrating that can be, but it is even worse when we shoot ourselves in the foot, as South did in this next example:

♠ A74
♡ J9863
◇ Q7
♣ KJ10

```
    N
  W   E
    S
```

♠ K63
♡ KQ104
◇ KJ6
♣ Q94

Contract 4♡ by South

South received the ♠J from West and won in hand with the king. With three 'top losers' it was crucial to his chances of success that no further losses were incurred, and that spade suit was worrying. He had to develop a trick, and quickly, to dispose of an impending spade loser.

Never mind, help was at hand, because diamonds provided him with precisely what he required. After knocking out the ace, he could discard a spade from dummy on ◇J, and then draw trumps. He rightly worked out that he could not play trumps first, or else the diamond suit would be established too slowly to be of any benefit.

He triumphantly led a diamond to dummy's queen, which held the trick! Strange, thought he, still, no matter, he continued the suit and West won his ace to continue spades. Declarer, perforce, had to win in dummy with the ace and then a sinking feeling came over him. He had a sorely needed diamond trick, but he could not reach it!

When he led a trump to try and reach his own hand, the defence pounced on it and cashed their spade winner. Declarer's ◇J could only watch the play from the sidelines.

What should declarer have done? He was entirely correct to sit back and plan the play, and due to this he was able to work out his overall strategy. Sadly it all came too late, because he deliberated after he had played from dummy at trick one. He had already made the fatal error.

To keep the entry to his hand, i e. where the last winning diamond was held, it was vital to win the opening lead in dummy, leaving ♠K intact. By thinking ahead, one should never be stranded as South was here.

That concludes the handling of trump contracts, but I will return to this theme in *Winning Bridge at Home* where I will be looking at more exotic techniques. Before I move on to 'no trump' play, the usual problems.

Quiz

1. In a trump contract, under what circumstances should you leave the drawing of trumps to later in the hand?

2. Do you normally look for ruffs in the short or long trump hand?

3. How do you define a 'cross-ruff'?

4. When would you establish a side-suit and what process is followed?

5. How would you play these four contracts?

(a)
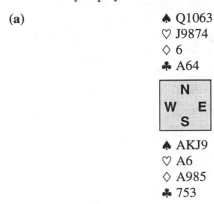

♠ Q1063
♡ J9874
♦ 6
♣ A64

♠ AKJ9
♡ A6
♦ A985
♣ 753

Contract 4♠ by South. Lead ♣K.

(b)
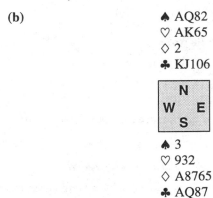

♠ AQ82
♡ AK65
♦ 2
♣ KJ106

♠ 3
♡ 932
♦ A8765
♣ AQ87

Contract 6♣ by South. Lead ♣3.

(c)

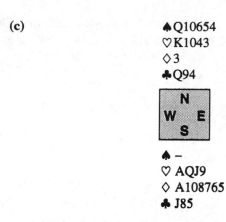

♠ Q10654
♡ K1043
◇ 3
♣ Q94

♠ –
♡ AQJ9
◇ A108765
♣ J85

Contract 4♡ by South. Lead ♠A.

(d)

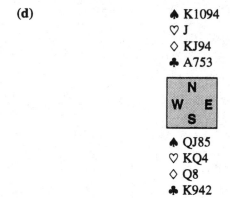

♠ K1094
♡ J
◇ KJ94
♣ A753

♠ QJ85
♡ KQ4
◇ Q8
♣ K942

Contract 4♠ by South. Lead ♣J.

Answers

1. You cannot afford to draw trumps if you:

    (a) need to produce extra tricks, or
    (b) will lose 'trump control', or
    (c) will remove all your trumps and cannot cash out immediately.

2. The short trump hand.

3. When you use your trumps in both hands independently.

4. When you require extra tricks. It is achieved by ruffing cards in the requisite suit, thus removing enemy high cards. The 'long winners' you hold will then enable you to discard losers from another suit.

5. (a)

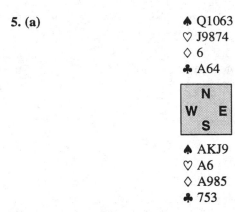

♠ Q1063
♡ J9874
◇ 6
♣ A64

♠ AKJ9
♡ A6
◇ A985
♣ 753

Contract 4♠ by South. Lead ♣K.

The play should go as follows. Win ♣A in dummy and lead a diamond to the ace. Ruff a diamond with ♠3 and lead a heart to South's ace. Again, ruff a diamond (ideally with ♠10, so you cannot be over-ruffed) and continue with ♠6 to South's ♠9. Finally, ruff South's last diamond in dummy with ♠Q.

You have collected seven tricks already and with ♠AKJ, you are assured of three more. Any other line risks defeat as the actual hand demonstrates:

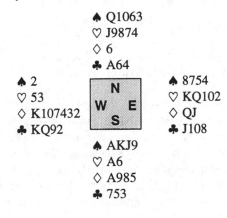

♠ Q1063
♡ J9874
◇ 6
♣ A64

♠ 2
♡ 53
◇ K107432
♣ KQ92

♠ 8754
♡ KQ102
◇ QJ
♣ J108

♠ AKJ9
♡ A6
◇ A985
♣ 753

5. (b)

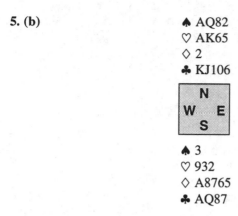

♠ AQ82
♡ AK65
◇ 2
♣ KJ106

♠ 3
♡ 932
◇ A8765
♣ AQ87

Contract 6♣ by South. Lead ♣3

As soon as you see a situation in which both hands have short suits opposite aces, you should immediately be thinking 'cross-ruff'. We manufacture an extra trick every time we take a ruff in each hand.

How do we calculate whether a cross-ruff will make the contract? The answer lies in the number of top tricks we possess outside trumps as the following calculation will show:

Tricks required to make 6♣			= 12
Top Tricks: Spades	Ace	= 1	
Hearts	Ace & King	= 2	
Diamonds	Ace	= 1	
Therefore tricks needed from trumps		**= 8**	

Originally, we needed to make all eight of our trumps separately. Unfortunately, West has made a distinct nuisance of himself by leading a trump at trick one, and hence we 'lose' one of the extra tricks. We are now one trick short and the only hope of salvation is the spade finesse. Despite holding a singleton spade in the South hand, we must nevertheless risk a loser in the suit, in order to obtain the crucial extra winner that West has denied us with his excellent opening lead.

Thus we proceed as follows. Win the lead in South and play a spade to the queen (close your eyes is an optional extra). Upon opening one's eyes, we see that East has not produced ♠K, so we are in business. Next we cash ♠A, ♡A and ♡K and lead a diamond to the ace. Why the mad rush to take our tricks?

The reason is that, whilst we continue on our cross-ruff, we do not want our opponents discarding in a suit where they may be able to ruff one of our top tricks. To illustrate this, let me break off for a moment and put in an example of East/West hands:

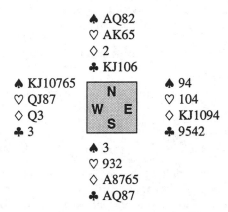

                    ♠ AQ82
                    ♡ AK65
                    ◇ 2
                    ♣ KJ106
    ♠ KJ10765   ♠ 94
    ♡ QJ87   ♡ 104
    ◇ Q3   ◇ KJ1094
    ♣ 3   ♣ 9542
                    ♠ 3
                    ♡ 932
                    ◇ A8765
                    ♣ AQ87

Hurricane Harry plays all his hands at the speed of light, mainly to show off and impress his opponents. As soon as dummy goes down, he realises that the spade finesse is required to succeed in the contract. When it works, he cashes ♠A and ruffs a spade while East, who does not follow to the third round of Spades, discards ♡4.

When he later comes to cash ♡AK, he will bemoan his luck, because East will ruff the king, denying him one of his winners. Had he cashed ♡AK before ruffing a Spade, he would have been safe. Back to the example.

Once we have safely collected all our aces and kings, we simply cross-ruff, leading diamonds from South and spades from North. East/West will take the final trick.

5. (c)

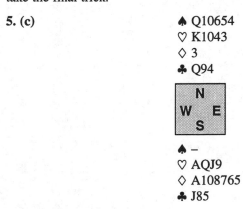

                    ♠ Q10654
                    ♡ K1043
                    ◇ 3
                    ♣ Q94

                    ♠ —
                    ♡ AQJ9
                    ◇ A108765
                    ♣ J85

Contract 4♡ by South. Lead ♠A

'What are we doing in 4♡', you may well ask, 'with only 12 points in the South hand and a meagre 7 in dummy?' We are out-gunned. At such times, it is always worth bearing in mind the power of having distributional hands allied to sufficient trumps.

We first examine our 'menu' of options:

1. *Can we draw trumps?*
No, because we do not have sufficient tricks afterwards.

2. *Can we cross-ruff?*
No, because we have only one top trick (♢A) allied to a maximum of eight trump tricks.

3. *Can we establish a suit?*
Yes, diamonds could be established with a bit of luck.

When we are in a poor contract, as here, we should visualise how the cards need to sit, and then play for that distribution. It is completely the opposite thinking to when our contract appears safe. The key to success on this hand will be establishing extra tricks in diamonds and we set about that straight away.

We ruff West's ♠A, cash ♢A and ruff a diamond in dummy. We cannot afford to ruff anything in the South hand, as it would reduce our trumps to two and one opponent will have three or more. We would have lost 'trump control', i.e. one opponent will have more than either declarer or dummy, and would be unable to draw trumps at any stage.

We, therefore, continue with a heart to the jack and a further diamond ruff. It is time to look at the full hand and assess our progress:

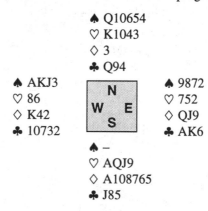

♠ Q10654
♡ K1043
♢ 3
♣ Q94

♠ AKJ3
♡ 86
♢ K42
♣ 10732

♠ 9872
♡ 752
♢ QJ9
♣ AK6

♠ —
♡ AQJ9
♢ A108765
♣ J85

Lo and behold, our second ruff removes all the East/West diamonds (the suit originally dividing 3-3, as indeed it had to do). We now return to hand in trumps and note both opponents follow. Nearly there. We draw the outstanding trump and enjoy three 'long' diamonds. In all, we have ten tricks, made up of:

4	Trumps in South
2	Ruffs in North (on diamonds)
1	◇ A
3	Long diamonds
10	

Game on 19 points – whatever next?!

5. (d)

<pre>
              ♠ K1094
              ♡ J
              ◇ KJ94
              ♣ A753

                  N
              W   E
                  S

              ♠ QJ85
              ♡ KQ4
              ◇ Q8
              ♣ K942
</pre>

Our final example demonstrating 'when we do not draw trumps' features South playing 4♠ on the lead of ♣J. Where are our losers?

1	in spades
1	in hearts
1	in diamonds
1	in clubs
4	

We have four losers if we draw trumps, so we must seek another route. With no prospect of a cross-ruff anywhere to be seen, nor a suit to establish long tricks in, we look to our last refuge – 'quick discards'.

Do we have a suit where we can quickly establish tricks to throw some losers away? We have two candidates, hearts and diamonds.

If we select diamonds and 'knock-out' the opponent's ace, we will have established two tricks (we require one of the KQJ to dislodge the ace, so we will have two remaining). That will give us one discard, as we must follow suit to the 'first' winner. One discard, however, is no use to us, for if we pitch either a heart, somewhat pointlessly, or better a club, we will still have a loser in the suit. We *need* two discards.

Hearts oblige us by providing the same two established tricks (king and queen) and the ability to discard on both of them. By throwing two clubs from the North hand, our loser will have disappeared.

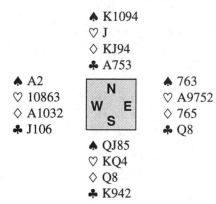

```
                    ♠ K1094
                    ♡ J
                    ◇ KJ94
                    ♣ A753
  ♠ A2                              ♠ 763
  ♡ 10863          N                ♡ A9752
  ◇ A1032       W     E             ◇ 765
  ♣ J106           S                ♣ Q8
                    ♠ QJ85
                    ♡ KQ4
                    ◇ Q8
                    ♣ K942
```

One cautionary note before leaving this deal. Do you spot a trap? What would happen if we won the first trick with ♣K? When the opponents have collected their ♡A and continued clubs, we would be stuck in dummy. Although we have set up our tricks, we could not get at them – most frustrating!

So remember, when seeking to take quick discards, always be sure to leave an entry to the hand where the tricks are contained. Here, it is South who has ♡KQ so it is his club honour which must remain intact. Win the opening lead with ♣A.

2
PLAYING NO TRUMP CONTRACTS

Introduction and Objectives

You would logically think that declaring no trumps would be less complex than playing suit contracts. After all, worrying about trumps is just another headache for an already furrowed brow. Without that diversion, surely life is easier?

Is it possible, then, to summarise our objectives when declaring no trump contracts in a clear and concise way? That would be the ideal of course. As a preliminary, we need to carefully examine two distinctly different approaches to the play.

The Hare
When the opponents attack their longest suit, the play in a no trump contract will often resemble a race. We need to be Linford Christie in these situations, for example:

```
            ♠ 3
            ♡ KQ4
            ◇ K9865
            ♣ K1094

          N
        W   E
          S

            ♠ AK4
            ♡ A5
            ◇ Q1042
            ♣ QJ85
```

Contract 3NT by South. Lead ♠5.

In our 3NT contract, the defenders make their best opening lead (as they always tend to do in books, although you will be pleased to hear that this is far from true at the bridge table).

Our initial action, in *any* contract, should be to review prospects and make a plan of campaign. We begin with analysing our top tricks, and we have five of those. We need an additional four. In clubs we have three establishable tricks and we have one in diamonds. At first glance we should have no difficulty achieving our contract.

However, we need also to consider the debit side of the balance sheet. What about our losers? Inevitably the minor suit aces will be lost, and our only other worry will be spades. After the ace and king have been dislodged, the opponents will have at least three tricks to take in the suit. Added to our top losers, that will defeat us.

In effect, both sides are playing the same game. Starting with their top winners and developing other tricks to go with them. The 'race' is on – who will get to the chequered flag first?

To answer this question, we must do a small calculation based on the following formula: *'The number of cards to dislodge must not exceed the number of 'stops' remaining in the opponents' suit'*.

Let us see how this works in practice. We have two stops in spades and we have two aces to dislodge. That would be okay if West had led a heart, say. However, we must perform our calculation after the first trick has been completed, and not before. At this point, we will have only one spade stop left, because one has been removed in dealing with the opening lead.

So, at the end of trick one, we have one spade stop *left*, but two aces to dislodge. Disaster! If we follow the 'normal' course of action and develop our tricks by starting with the most attractive proposition, i.e. clubs, we will be defeated. Do we have any chance at all?

Diamonds provide some hope, for if the suit behaves kindly we might win the four tricks we require without needing to touch clubs at all. If we could achieve this, we would balance our equation, because it would be necessary to dislodge only one card, $\diamond$A, before we had nine tricks. Therefore, we must ignore the apparent warmth and safety of tackling clubs and go out into the cold, harsh world of diamonds.

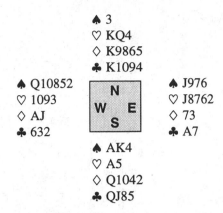

♠ 3
♡ KQ4
◊ K9865
♣ K1094

♠ Q10852   ♠ J976
♡ 1093   ♡ J8762
◊ AJ   ◊ 73
♣ 632   ♣ A7

♠ AK4
♡ A5
◊ Q1042
♣ QJ85

As the opposing cards lie favourably for us, we will achieve our goal and secure the four diamond tricks we require for success. We win ♠ K at trick one and play ◊ 2. West wins his ace and returns another spade, driving out our final stop in the suit.

However, we can now cash our diamonds and hearts immediately and, by the time we come to play on clubs, we already have nine tricks neatly stacked up in front of us. Or, put another way, we won the race to be first across the line.

Had we played on clubs at trick two instead of diamonds, the opponents would again continue spades. After taking our three club tricks, we would still need four more. With only three top tricks (in hearts), we cannot 'cash-out', and therefore play a diamond. Before we are allowed to win the trick we require, West grabs ◊ A and takes his three spade tricks. We are defeated, because our line of play was too 'slow'. We lost the race.

The Tortoise
Not every no trump hand mirrors a race to the line, otherwise the much-heralded complexity and fascination of the game would be hard to find. The extreme opposite of the 'hare' is as you would expect, the 'tortoise'. Let me show you an example:

Dealer South. Game All.

♠ AQJ7
♡ K4
◇ Q98
♣ Q1082

♠ K42
♡ AJ10
◇ K1042
♣ J97

West	North	East	South
–	–	–	1NT(i)
Pass	3NT	Pass	Pass
Pass			

(i)   The so-called 'weak' no trump, showing between 12 and 14 points and a balanced hand (see Chapter 7 on 'Range of 1NT Openings')

Against our 3NT contract, West chooses the lead of ♠10 and we assess our prospects. We have six top tricks and can easily establish one in diamonds. If we guessed who had ◇J, we would have three tricks in the suit and our contract. If in racing mode, that is what we would do.

An alternative option is to play on clubs, which will ultimately win us two tricks in the suit. Together with one in diamonds and our top tricks, that will be enough for our contract. However, it is a slow process and we need to ask ourselves, 'Do we have time for all of this?'

The answer is 'yes', we do, because our opponents have led a safe or passive card which although not giving anything to us directly, does provide time to develop our tricks. This situation is best described as the 'tortoise', i.e. no one is in a hurry, but we will reach the finishing line eventually. This time, we will beat the hare who rushes to find quick tricks, only to lose five and his contract, on the way.

Establishing Tricks

The ability to establish extra tricks, without creating additional losers is fundamental to declarer play. Let us look at some of the more effective ways of making tricks from straw.

High Cards
The easiest way to develop a trick is to drive out the opposition's top cards in a suit where we have length and minor honours:

♠ Q1084
♡ AQ4
◇ AJ9
♣ 1083

♠ J95
♡ K52
◇ Q842
♣ QJ7

South declares 1NT and West leads ♣4 (the fourth highest, see Chapter 3 on 'Opening Leads') which runs to your seven. You have three tricks on top in hearts, one in diamonds and you have collected a club. You should now attack spades to develop the extra two winners you need, rather than go after diamonds. Remember:

Established tricks = Length of longest suit minus number of top tricks the opposition holds, provided you have at least four consecutive 'honours' (see *Play Bridge at Home* for a more detailed analysis).

Finesses
Sometimes we have a suit to develop which requires a finesse. Let us move a '10' in the previous example to see how it changes our approach to the hand:

♠ Q842
♡ AQ4
◇ AJ9
♣ 1083

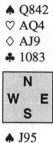

♠ J95
♡ K52
◇ Q1084
♣ QJ7

Again, the lead is ♣4 coming round to your 7, but on this occasion we have no easy continuation in spades, because one of the key 'intermediates' is missing. We must now look to diamonds and develop tricks there, two more if the finesse fails; maybe three when it succeeds.

Sometimes we must finesse when we do not have top cards in a suit, for example:

♠ K1084
♡ AQ4
◇ AJ9
♣ 1083

♠ J95
♡ K52
◇ Q842
♣ QJ7

Back in 1NT again on the same lead, we turn our attention to spades because of the solidity of our intermediates (we hold the J1098). How many tricks can we expect to develop in the suit?

If West has ♠Q, we will take three tricks in the suit, if not, we will have to settle for two. Either way, we have not added to our losers, and can still hope to succeed in the contract.

Long Suits

A no trump contract has less variety than suit play because the development of tricks is one-dimensional, i.e. there are no trumps to confuse us. The underlying concept of declaring or defending no trumps is 'You play your suit and we'll play ours'. This comes about because long cards in a suit *will* become tricks because *they cannot be ruffed*. For example:

♠ KJ4
♡ Q107
◇ A9753
♣ K4

♠ A95
♡ AK4
◇ 864
♣ A853

North/South arrive in 3NT with South as declarer, and receive the lead of the ♡2. First, our South must decide if it is a 'hare' or a 'tortoise' hand but, with three stops in hearts, that does not take him long.

A quick scan of top tricks reveals has eight, so one more needed. If there was urgency required South could finesse in spades, giving a 50% chance of success, but such drastic measures are not required. With a preponderance of diamonds between the hands declarer knows that there is a source of tricks. So declarer tackles that suit in preference to spades, and quite right too.

Assuming the opposing diamonds divide 'evenly' (i.e. 3-2), another two tricks will eventually be created. As a brief test, how many tricks will you *establish* in the following examples:

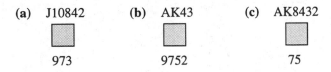

(a) J10842	(b) AK43	(c) AK8432
973	9752	75

The answers are:

(a) 2

(b) 1 These are added to your 'top tricks' to get the total

(c) 3 tricks in the suit, i.e. (b) = 3 (c) = 5

Quiz

Before we move on to other more advanced techniques for finding those extra tricks, try these three play problems first:

1.

        ♠ A3
        ♡ K74
        ♢ Q10985
        ♣ J104

        ♠ K92
        ♡ AQJ6
        ♢ J7
        ♣ KQ92

Contract 3NT by South. Lead ♠4.

2.

        ♠ KQ4
        ♡ 73
        ♢ AQ84
        ♣ Q987

        ♠ J1083
        ♡ A4
        ♢ 1097
        ♣ AKJ4

Contract 3NT by South. Lead ♡K.

3.

♠ AJ4
♡ 1073
◊ A842
♣ 1073

♠ KQ62
♡ AJ5
◊ 973
♣ Q82

Contract 1NT by South. Lead ♠10.

Answers

1.

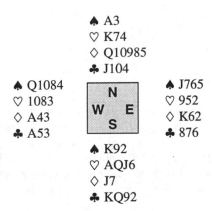

♠ A3
♡ K74
◊ Q10985
♣ J104

♠ Q1084   ♠ J765
♡ 1083   ♡ 952
◊ A43   ◊ K62
♣ A53   ♣ 876

♠ K92
♡ AQJ6
◊ J7
♣ KQ92

We have six top tricks in the majors, and thus require three more. We can develop tricks in either diamonds or clubs, and both will produce exactly the three tricks we require. Does it matter, then, which suit we attack?

There would not be much point to the problem if the answer to that question was 'No', and the key factor is time. In clubs we give up the lead once (to ♣A), whereas in diamonds we would have to concede two tricks. With only one spade stop left we cannot afford that luxury.

So win the opening lead, and immediately play ♣J (lead honours from the shorter suit first, remember) and continue with clubs upon regaining the lead. Then cash the hearts and smile sweetly at the opponents (an optional extra, but always recommended!).

2.

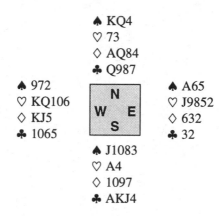

♠ KQ4
♡ 73
◇ AQ84
♣ Q987

♠ 972
♡ KQ106
◇ KJ5
♣ 1065

♠ A65
♡ J9852
◇ 632
♣ 32

♠ J1083
♡ A4
◇ 1097
♣ AKJ4

West leads ♡K against our 3NT contract, thus removing our only stop. As with problem one, we have six top tricks and need three more, and at first glance the spade suit appears ideal for the purpose. However, if we tackle the suit, East/West will be able to win ♠A and take at least four hearts, defeating our contract.

Of course, sometimes no successful route exists and we have to accept our minus score as graciously as possible. However, in general, it is always worth trying anything, however unlikely, which may bring us success. This is not only because the rewards greatly outweigh the price of failure, but also because the most thrilling bridge hands tend to be those which succeed when having no apparent chance of doing so.

Here, our attention must turn to diamonds – can we establish three extra winners *immediately* i.e. take four 'top' tricks? There is a chance, for if West holds both the king *and* jack of the suit, we could 'double finesse'. In other words, we win the heart and follow with ◇10. If West plays low, so do we, although more in hope than expectation.

If East cannot beat ◇10, as on the actual layout, we will win the trick. We repeat the finesse 'covering' whatever card West plays i.e. playing the queen on the jack or the ace on the king.

In this way we will take four diamond tricks to go with four clubs and a heart. We only had a 25% chance (1 in 4 that West would have both key cards) but we gambled on that and won!

3.

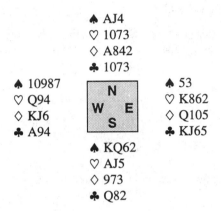

♠ AJ4
♥ 1073
♦ A842
♣ 1073

♠ 10987
♥ Q94
♦ KJ6
♣ A94

♠ 53
♥ K862
♦ Q105
♣ KJ65

♠ KQ62
♥ AJ5
♦ 973
♣ Q82

Contract 1NT by South. Lead ♠ 10.

Against our modest 1NT contract, West finds a non-threatening spade lead which does not to help us. Our top tricks come to six, so one more is needed, which suit should we attack? Let us examine our options:

1. Hearts
If East has ♥ K and ♥ Q we will establish a second trick in the suit, so we have a 25% chance there.

2. Diamonds
If the opposing diamonds divide 3-3, we will eventually establish a second trick in the suit to go with ♦ A. A 3-3 division is slightly better than a 1 in 3 chance (35%).

3. Clubs
If East has ♣ AK and we lead the suit from dummy, our queen cannot be denied her moment of supremacy. Again 25%.

So on a purely mathematical basis we should tackle diamonds, but we cannot carry a calculator at the table, so these small differences in odds are hard to determine. Is there an easier way of thinking about the hand?

What we should consider is the other side of the coin. We should ask ourselves the following questions:

(a) Which suit offers the greatest security?
(b) Which suit does not create 'additional' losers?

The answer to the first question is usually the suit with the most cards held between the two hands. That gives the opponents less possible winners to take if the suit behaves badly.

The second question is more about whether your opponents actually benefit by you touching a suit first. To show this more clearly, look at the heart suit again:

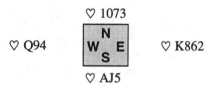

$\heartsuit$ 1073

$\heartsuit$ Q94 $\heartsuit$ K862

$\heartsuit$ AJ5

We will consider how many tricks each side would win if they broached the suit *first:*

1. North

Lead a low heart to South's jack and West's queen. We later lay down $\heartsuit$ A in the hope that the king falls. No such luck. One trick to North/South.

2. South

We lead a low heart to North's 10 and East's king. Later we cross to North to lead to the jack, but West produces $\heartsuit$ Q. One trick to North/South.

So, if we tackle the suit as North/South, we win the trick we always had, $\heartsuit$ A. However:

3. East

Leads a low heart to partner's queen, but South retains $\heartsuit$ AJ over the king. South can later finesse $\heartsuit$ J, or if West returns the suit this will not be necessary. Two tricks to North/South.

4. West

Leads a low heart to partner's king and South's ace. North/South possess both the $\heartsuit$ 10 and $\heartsuit$ J and must win one further trick in the suit. Two tricks to North/South.

In other words, whoever starts playing hearts will 'lose' a trick.

No such problem exists for South if he decides to search for his extra trick in diamonds. It makes no difference whatsoever who *breaks* the suit, because all the minor honours and intermediates (i.e. QJ10) are held by the same side. In that circumstance a suit will be 'safe'.

When the East/West diamonds divide 3-3, South will make a second trick in the suit. If they do not, nothing will have been achieved, but nothing given away either. Such is the nature of the 'tortoise'. Slow but sure.

So, returning to our problem, we should win the spade and immediately play diamonds. On regaining the lead, we continue the suit setting up the 'thirteenth' in dummy – our seventh trick. In the meantime, our opponents are forced to continue spades, for a switch to any other suit will give us the extra trick we are looking for. They are snookered.

More Advanced Techniques

Whilst a grounding in the basics of card play is essential, it is not sufficient for us to progress to a good standard. More advanced techniques are required.

It would be all too easy for me to get carried away in this chapter and deal with esoteric or unusual card play manoeuvres which, whilst being dazzling and exciting in nature, do not arise frequently enough at the table to make them worthwhile. What I want to do is to focus on good practical advances in play rather than go straight in at the deep end. I can't swim anyway!

Going from Hand to Hand
Here are two suits possessed by you and dummy:

Dummy
♠ AQJ
♡ 743

N
W E
S

♠ 875
♡ KQ5
Declarer

For the sake of this example, we will ignore the rest of the hand. I have already said that we should always strive to lead towards honours, rather than away from them, but how do we arrange that in practice? In the example, let us assume that we are currently in declarer's hand; should we lead spades or hearts? The answer is that from declarer's side, spade leads are best, but from dummy we should tackle hearts.

Therefore, lead a spade to the jack and, if it holds the trick, continue with a heart towards ♡KQ. If an honour wins, repeat the spade finesse, and then go back to hearts once more.

The lead has bounced backwards and forwards between declarer and dummy over the four tricks.

Moving on, how would you tackle this 3NT contract?

Dealer West. North/South Game.

```
              ♠ AK
              ♡ 1087
              ◊ J8743
              ♣ 1075
         ┌─────────┐
         │    N    │
         │  W   E  │
         │    S    │
         └─────────┘
              ♠ Q875
              ♡ A53
              ◊ A6
              ♣ AQJ4
```

West	North	East	South
Pass	Pass	1♡	1NT
Pass	2NT	Pass	3NT
Pass	Pass	Pass	

West leads ♡9, you cover with the 10 in dummy, just in case something extraordinary happens, East plays the jack and you win the ace. It is critical that you handle the movement between hands completely accurately. Formulate your plan before reading on.

First play a spade to dummy's king, then lead a low club to the jack, which we expect to hold the trick (as East opened the bidding). Then back to dummy in spades before another *low* club (in case East has ♣Kx) to the queen. Then cash our winners.

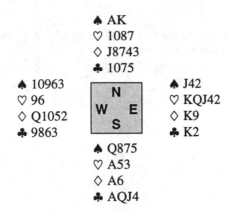

                    ♠ AK
                    ♡ 1087
                    ◊ J8743
                    ♣ 1075

♠ 10963   ♠ J42
♡ 96   ♡ KQJ42
◊ Q1052   ◊ K9
♣ 9863   ♣ K2

                    ♠ Q875
                    ♡ A53
                    ◊ A6
                    ♣ AQJ4

Sometimes we have to be careful to take our tricks in the right order, for example:

                    ♠ AQ
                    ♡ QJ53
                    ◊ J986
                    ♣ 1075

                    ♠ KJ107
                    ♡ AK
                    ◊ 10752
                    ♣ A42

Contract 3NT by South. Lead ♣3.

Again, we are in 3NT and the opposition (as usual) find the best lead of a club to the king and ace. We must cash our major suits correctly by first taking ♡AK, then playing a spade to the *ace*. In dummy for the last time, we continue with our heart winners before playing ♠Q and *overtaking with the king*. Now we can enjoy two more spade tricks and make our contract.

You will see the movement from hand to hand crop up repeatedly, and you will develop an instinct for being in the right place at the right time. And if you don't, see me after school!

Entries

The use of entries is very much associated with 'going from hand to hand' in that an entry enables you to reach the other side (of the bridge ...). Here is an example of using entries correctly:

♠ 765
♡ J2
◇ Q109862
♣ KQ

♠ AK43
♡ Q875
◇ KJ4
♣ A7

Contract 3NT by South. Lead ♣3.

As soon as we see a situation where one hand has a long suit, and thus particularly in no trumps, the potential to win many tricks, we must always jealously guard the entry situation. The key is to *preserve entries in the hand with the winners*.

Here, that hand is North, with its lovely array of diamonds, but entries are scarce. If we allow dummy to win the first trick with ♣Q, and the defenders refuse to take their ◇A on the first two rounds of the suit (see 'hold-up play' below), all those winners will stare at us for the rest of the hand. No doubt they will be saying 'serves you right for not thinking at trick one'!

Had we carefully won ♣A (overtaking the queen) we could not have been denied entry to our winners later in the play. We would have unblocked the clubs, and kept the top card in dummy, where it needed to be.

Hold-up Play

Consider this hand:

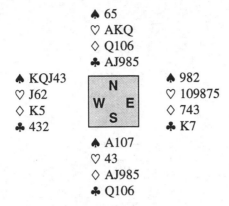

```
                 ♠ 65
                 ♡ AKQ
                 ◇ Q106
                 ♣ AJ985
    ♠ KQJ43        N        ♠ 982
    ♡ J62                    ♡ 109875
    ◇ K5      W       E      ◇ 743
    ♣ 432         S          ♣ K7
                 ♠ A107
                 ♡ 43
                 ◇ AJ985
                 ♣ Q106
```

Contract 3NT by South. Lead ♠K.

West leads ♠K and up until now we have always won straight away with the ace, and gone about our business. All that is about to change, because we are now going to discover the 'hold-up'.

Let us consider what would happen if we played the 'old way'. Winning ♠A at trick one, we would choose a finesse to take in one of the minors, but this time they both fail. As soon as either opponent gets in, a torrent of spade winners will follow and our contract is defeated.

Incidentally, bridge players always seem desperate to check if the 'other' finesse would have worked, and seeing that it didn't satisfy themselves that the contract had no chance. They would be very wrong, for 3NT is almost 100% certain to make if played correctly.

Instead of winning ♠A at trick one, let us try the effect of taking it at the last possible moment. What are we achieving by that, you may ask? Simply this. If we wait until trick three, and then take a club finesse to East, which of course loses, he has no more spades to play. West could defeat us if he had the lead, but he hasn't. You have starved the defenders of the means to go from hand to hand, i.e. East cannot reach West.

Should East now play a diamond, you must rise with the ace and cash your nine tricks (one spade, three hearts, one diamond and four clubs). By holding up your ♠A until the third round of the suit, you exhausted East of his spades and, with it, the only way to get to his partner's hand.

Avoidance Play

Go back to the last hand a moment and consider it without the East/West cards:

♠ 65
♡ AKQ
◇ Q106
♣ AJ985

```
    N
 W     E
    S
```

♠ A107
♡ 43
◇ AJ985
♣ Q106

Contract 3NT by South. Lead of ♠K.

After taking ♠A on the third round, should we finesse in clubs or diamonds? If our finesse succeeds we have at least ten tricks, but unfortunately we do not know which one will work. What happens if we choose one which fails (as I invariably tend to do in such circumstances)? Does it matter which suit is tackled?

We have to ask ourselves whether we have a preference for which opponent we would rather have on lead. If we do, we should arrange our play to ensure that the 'danger' hand is kept out. On this deal we must *avoid West getting in* and cashing his long spades, so the finesse must lose to East. Hence we select clubs rather than diamonds, knowing heads we win and tails they lose. Think of West as carrying a label saying 'danger keep out'.

Before we leave declarer play and move on to defence, one final word of advice. Many mistakes are made early in the hand. There is nothing more annoying to me than realising half way through the play that, had I done something different earlier, the contract would now be simple. Whereas I am now struggling away, often to no avail.

Planning, strategy, call it what you will – the crucial phrase is *'Think at trick one'*. An error is all too easily made if you 'react' to dummy, e.g. with delight that your contract looks okay, or more often in my experience, with disappointment that a disaster looms. It is then that our eye is taken off the ball, for example:

♠ A432
♡ K4
◇ AK
♣ A10873

♠ J65
♡ AJ3
◇ QJ1084
♣ 42

Contract 3NT by South. Lead of ♡2.

You arrive in 3NT and West leads a low heart round to your ♡AJ. You play low from dummy and win East's queen with your ace. When you cash ◇AK everyone follows and then you see a snag: how do you get back to South to take the rest of the diamonds? The sad answer is that you can't, unless your opponents are nice to you. What could be done?

Back to trick one, and we must first see how many tricks we have. Two black aces, ♡ AK and five diamonds give us nine 'on top', we do not need an extra heart. Furthermore, we should have spotted that our winners were in the weaker hand, so we need to preserve any entry to them. Hence, rise with ♡K at trick one, cash ◇AK and then come to ♡A to take the balance of the diamonds. Easy when we sit back and think for a moment, but just as easy to go wrong.

Quiz

Finally, three hands to test your play.

1. How do you plan to play this 3NT contract? West leads ♡3 to the king and …?

♠J7
♡1042
◇1073
♣A8753

♠A865
♡AQ5
◇AK2
♣K94

2. You reach 3NT by South after West has opened the bidding with 1◇. Lead ◇K. How do you plan the play?

♠Q87
♡A1094
◇73
♣KQ86

♠AJ10
♡J5
◇A82
♣AJ1074

3. Contract 1NT by South. Lead ♡3.How do you play?

♠984
♡K6
◇Q10943
♣743

♠Q1073
♡AJ
◇KJ8
♣A862

Answers

1.

♠ J7
♡ 1042
◇ 1073
♣ A8753

♠ 10432   ♠ KQ9
♡ J986   ♡ K73
◇ J65   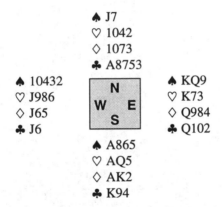   ◇ Q984
♣ J6   ♣ Q102

♠ A865
♡ AQ5
◇ AK2
♣ K94

You have seven top tricks after the opening lead, and need to develop two more. To play on clubs seems the obvious answer, but if you cash the ace and king of the suit, and concede a trick to East, how do you get back to dummy to enjoy those two lovely winners?

This kind of situation is a variation on the theme of entries, where the entry is in the suit itself. Hence, first cash ♣K, and then play another club, *ducking in dummy*. When you regain the lead, you can cross to dummy with ♣A and cash your winners. You need to preserve an entry *within the suit*.

Other examples where a duck may be necessary are:

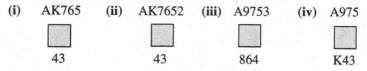

(i)   AK765   **(ii)**   AK7652   **(iii)**   A9753   **(iv)**   A975

       43   43   864   K43

There are many similar holdings, and they all have a couple of things in common:

   (a) You have the ace (and possibly king) of the suit in question.
   (b) You have at least one automatic or unavoidable loser before you
       can establish the suit.

In this situation, it rarely costs to duck a trick early in the play of the suit.

2.

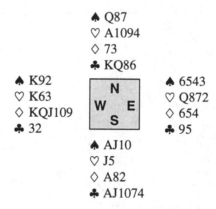

    ♠ Q87
    ♡ A1094
    ◊ 73
    ♣ KQ86

♠ K92   ♠ 6543
♡ K63   ♡ Q872
◊ KQJ109   ◊ 654
♣ 32   ♣ 95

    ♠ AJ10
    ♡ J5
    ◊ A82
    ♣ AJ1074

This example shows how two of our advanced techniques often go side by side. I hope you recognised the *ducking play* required at tricks one and two to starve East of his diamonds. Once East is the 'safe' player to have on lead, however, a second technique, that of *avoidance play,* comes to the fore.

With eight top tricks, you require only one more. You could take the spade finesse getting the hand over with quickly. If the finesse succeeds you have ten tricks, if it fails you have eight. The alternative is to tackle hearts. First you play a low heart to dummy's nine, which loses to East who will switch to a spade. Resisting the temptation to finesse in the light of West's opening bid, you rise with the Ace and continue with ♡J. Should West play low, you finesse once more, and will make your contract whenever West has one of the heart honours.

Although by no means certain to be successful, this line offers you the best chance. If the spade finesse had been through West, such pyrotechnics in hearts would not have been necessary.

3.

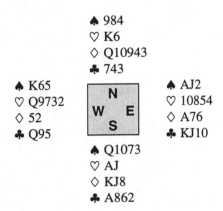

        ♠ 984
        ♡ K6
        ◇ Q10943
        ♣ 743

♠ K65   ♠ AJ2
♡ Q9732   ♡ 10854
◇ 52   ◇ A76
♣ Q95   ♣ KJ10

        ♠ Q1073
        ♡ AJ
        ◇ KJ8
        ♣ A862

A more modest contract of 1NT, but still there is a need to be vigilant. If you carelessly play a low heart from dummy and win East's ten with your jack (or if you rise with ♡K) you will live to regret it.

You can establish the diamonds but, if East withholds his Ace, how can you enjoy them? Make sure you win the first trick with ♡A keeping dummy's entry intact.

Please bear in mind the ducking play by East as a defender and how the objectives are identical to the hold-up by declarer. It is time for us to move to defending in all its glory ....

3
OPENING LEADS

Introduction

Which element of bridge would you think is generally regarded as the toughest?

(a) Declarer Play
(b) Bidding
(c) Defence

In fact, it is accepted wisdom that defence is the hardest part of the game by quite a distance. The reason why this is so, is a combination of factors:

1. You cannot see your partner's hand.
2. Your first move, the opening lead, is made before you see dummy.
3. Your margin of error is small, unlike bidding where often more than one contract may succeed.
4. Your partner may have ideas of his own!

The fourth of these points is, in many ways, one of the answers to being an effective defender. You must play *with* partner. It is rare indeed for two completely different lines of attack to be successful, so it is important to choose one and stick to it. Continually switching suits is a recipe for allowing contracts to make, and irritating partner simultaneously (I usually find one of those is much worse than the other!)

To develop a cohesive defensive strategy, I intend to start at the beginning and consider opening leads. If you believe that the opening lead is a minor part of defence (like the kick-off at soccer) let me assure you that more contracts are allowed to make because of a faulty or unlucky opening lead, than for *any* other reason.

Until now, the defence has always found the optimum opening lead in this book; now it's your turn. Our opening lead must achieve two totally different things:

1. It must be what we consider to be our best chance of defeating the contract.
2. It must tell our partner something about the suit we have led.

The first point is self-evident, although not quite as trivial as it might first appear. The second point re-affirms the commitment to defend together, i.e. this process begins with the defence's first card and continues throughout the hand.

Which Suit do We Lead?

Let us consider how we assess the 'best' chance of beating a contract. Here is an example hand:

♠ QJ4
♡ AK4
♢ J10932
♣ 43

What do you lead?

If you can answer that question already, then frankly I am amazed. In practice one cannot hope to judge what to lead on a hand until you know two things:

(a) The final contract
(b) The bidding

To support my statement, take our example hand and choose your lead against the following three contracts:

(a) 6NT
(b) 3NT
(c) 5♡

Against 6NT you can double and cash your two heart tricks, but that would achieve little against 3NT. There you need a strategy to develop five tricks. With two in hearts and potentially one in spades, a diamond lead offers the best chance of finding the other two.

Finally, needing three tricks against 5♡, a spade has great appeal aiming to establish one trick to go with your ♡AK.

As you can see, any notion that a hand is an island as regards choice of opening lead is misplaced. The final contract is critical to sensible selection. Not only that, but the bidding itself may give us a strong indication of what to do. Here you are West, and we have a couple of example sequences: which suit would you lead on each?

♠ AK43
♡ Q1086
◊ 10975
♣ 4

(a)

West	North	East	South
–	–	–	1♡
Pass	1♠	Pass	2♣
Pass	2♡	Pass	Pass
Pass			

(b)

West	North	East	South
–	–	–	1♠
Pass	2◊	Pass	2♡
Pass	2♠	Pass	Pass
Pass			

Both the sequences are superficially very similar in that they have finished in part-scores after North has returned his partner to his first bid suit. However, they introduce many of the *key factors in lead selection:*

1. Level of contract
2. 'Unbid suits'
3. Suits bid by declarer
4. Suits bid by partner
5. Suits bid by dummy
6. The bidding as a whole

How all these apparently diverse aspects come together will hopefully become clearer as we discuss the examples. Let us look at the first, *level of contract*.

The defence needs six tricks to succeed. What does this tell us? The most important fact is that time is on our side. Roughly translated this means that 'the more you have, the less hurry to take it'. When the opposition have rested in a low-level part score, with neither player showing any interest in a game contract, you can expect their combined strength to be approximately equal to yours.

In this type of situation, the defence needs to have, as its number one priority, the objective of giving nothing away. It needs to err on the side of safety or be passive in its approach to the early tricks, and leave the running to declarer. The beauty of having time is that, should you have started the defence in the wrong place, you will almost always have the opportunity to change tack.

With that in mind, I would plump for a *diamond* in bidding sequence (a), even though I am rejecting the opportunity to win the first trick with a spade. Against a higher-level contract, such as 4♡, I would prefer to lead ♠A in an effort to get a couple of tricks in the suit quickly, and then rely on my good trump holding to beat the contract. Different levels, different objectives, different leads:

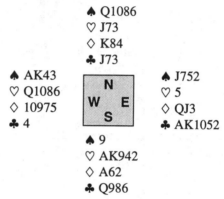

```
                    ♠ Q1086
                    ♡ J73
                    ◇ K84
                    ♣ J73
  ♠ AK43                          ♠ J752
  ♡ Q1086        N                ♡ 5
  ◇ 10975      W   E              ◇ QJ3
  ♣ 4            S                ♣ AK1052
                    ♠ 9
                    ♡ AK942
                    ◇ A62
                    ♣ Q986
```

Contract 2♡ by South.

In a part-score contract such as 2♡, the need for haste does not normally exist. A successful defence is only likely if you start with diamonds and stick with them until a trick is established. In 4♡ however, this may be the situation:

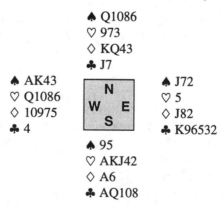

```
                    ♠ Q1086
                    ♡ 973
                    ◇ KQ43
                    ♣ J7
  ♠ AK43                          ♠ J72
  ♡ Q1086        N                ♡ 5
  ◇ 10975      W   E              ◇ J82
  ♣ 4            S                ♣ K96532
                    ♠ 95
                    ♡ AKJ42
                    ◇ A6
                    ♣ AQ108
```

Now the failure to cash our ♠AK at the first two tricks may result in the contract being allowed to make. One of our winners is in serious danger of 'running away', as declarer can discard a losing spade on dummy's ◊Q.

Note how the presence of extra high card strength enables North/South to discard losers, something which tends to happen rarely at lower levels.

Bidding sequence (b) sees a slight change in that the opponents are playing in spades rather than hearts and, the suits bid are different. This example allows us to examine a couple of further points regarding suit selection for opening leads.

It would be unusual to consider leading a heart because it is a *suit bid by declarer*. These suits are almost verboten. A suit bid by dummy, i.e. diamonds, is still very much in the picture however. Why is this?

To answer that question, look at these two layouts, with South as declarer, and West to lead:

(i)   973

          Q1086   N
                    W   E   52
                       S

                       AKJ4

(ii)   AKJ4

          52   N
                    W   E   Q1086
                       S

                       973

In (i), it is quite probable that South has mentioned this suit during the bidding. If we lead 'away from our queen', declarer will scoop in a cheap trick with his jack. In effect we have given a trick away, because our queen was 'off-side', i.e. 'over' declarer, and any finesse would fail.

In (ii) let us assume dummy has bid this suit. This completely reverses the orientation of the high cards, so that although the queen is still 'off side', leading the suit does not affect its chances of winning a trick. We now have a safe, if somewhat undynamic, selection.

It is easy to see how layout (i) could be the division of hearts in example (b).

We are left with *clubs,* the old faithful 'unbid' suit. The *unbid suit* has, throughout the life of bridge, been a popular choice for opening leads. The underlying reason is that the bidding tends to announce where players have strength (and length) in their hands. If a suit has been left out, i.e. not bid at any stage, isn't it logical to assume a deficiency in that department?

Take this West hand and consider what you lead against the following sequences:

$$\spadesuit \text{ J109}$$
$$\heartsuit \text{ J109}$$
$$\diamondsuit \text{ J109}$$
$$\clubsuit \text{ 8765}$$

(a)

West	North	East	South
–	–	–	1♡
Pass	2♣	Pass	2◇
Pass	3♣	Pass	3NT
Pass	Pass	Pass	

(b)

West	North	East	South
–	–	–	1♠
Pass	2♣	Pass	2◇
Pass	3♣	Pass	3NT
Pass	Pass	Pass	

(c)

West	North	East	South
–	–	–	1♠
Pass	2♣	Pass	2♡
Pass	3♣	Pass	3NT
Pass	Pass	Pass	

Did you select:

  (a) ♠
  (b) ♡
  (c) ◇ ?

Your reasoning should include some of the following points:

1. North has repeated his clubs and I would expect that to be a source of tricks in 3NT. Not a good place to attack.

2. Declarer has bid two suits, and will probably have a little support in clubs as well, leaving him with very few cards in the 'fourth suit'.

3. With only three points it is important that I deliver a lead my partner will like, because we are relying on him to find enough tricks to beat the contract.

4. As it is a game we are defending, a passive lead is less likely to work.

A lot to consider, but then, as a defender or potential defender, one should always be listening carefully to the bidding and trying to determine what the opponents have. After all they are telling each other, so why shouldn't you listen in? You will not go far wrong in any defensive situation if you always keep the bidding, and what it shows, in mind.

Quiz

Before we move on to which card you lead, a little test (you are always West) on which suit to lead:

1. ♠ 9873

    ♡ AQ92

    ◇ 73

    ♣ J94

West	North	East	South
–	–	–	1NT
Pass	Pass	Pass	

2. ♠ 62

    ♡ 1074

    ◇ AJ93

    ♣ KJ84

West	North	East	South
–	–	–	1♡
Pass	1♠	Pass	2◇
Pass	2♡	Pass	3♡
Pass	4♡	Pass	Pass
Pass			

3. ♠ Q1052

    ♡ 93

    ◇ A73

    ♣ Q1052

West	North	East	South
–	–	–	1◇
Pass	1♡	Pass	2♡
Pass	3◇	Pass	3NT
Pass	Pass	Pass	

4. ♠ 96

    ♡ K10763

    ◇ J10763

    ♣ 9

West	North	East	South
–	–	1♠	2♣
Pass	2◇	Pass	2NT
Pass	3NT	Pass	Pass
Pass			

5.	♠ A743	West	North	East	South
	♡ A	–	–	–	1♡
	◇ 9873	Pass	2◇	Pass	3◇
	♣ 6543	Pass	3♡	Pass	4♡
		Pass	Pass	Pass	

6.	♠ 85	West	North	East	South
	♡ J1084	–	–	–	1♠
	◇ KJ95	Pass	2♣	Pass	2♠
	♣ Q106	Pass	4♠	Pass	Pass
		Pass			

Answers

1. A spade

Although the heart suit is stronger, the danger of allowing declarer, who is the most likely holder of ♡K, to win a cheap trick, suggests a more cautious approach is best. Note that we are defending a part score, and thus we eye the passive lead with more enthusiasm. Just change things a little, though, and the conclusion is different, for example:

♠ 9873	West	North	East	South
♡ KJ92	–	–	–	1NT
◇ 73	Pass	3NT	Pass	Pass
♣ J94	Pass			

My recommendation would now be for a heart lead, because there is more emphasis on speed once North has announced strength. True, you could easily give a trick away, that is the nature of an 'active' lead, but the hope is that it will rarely be a decisive one, i.e. it will be an overtrick. In return, you start the defence in the place which is most likely to hurt declarer.

2. A heart

A trump lead is often wrongly criticised and seriously undervalued by experts. 'Only lead a trump if you can't think of anything else' is a well known phrase. However, if used propitiously a trump attack can be a valuable weapon in your arsenal. When is the *right time to lead a trump?* There are certain clues we should search for:

1. The opponents are in a suit which has been *bid and supported* but remain in a part score.
2. When declarer has bid a second suit (not trumps) and you have a good holding in that suit.

3. When your holding in the unbid suit is unattractive to lead from.
4. When there is no unbid suit.
5. When your trump holding is three (or more) little cards.
6. When your holding in dummy's suit suggests that partner is well capable of dealing with its threat.

Of course, it is impossible to find a hand where all six pointers apply but, should you detect a situation which has three or more of the above, it may well be time to lead a trump. Time to look at the problem again, and see how a trump fares:

1. Not true, they are in game.
2. *True,* your diamonds are ideal for a trump lead.
3. *True,* leading aces without a purpose is very dangerous.
4. Not true, clubs are unbid.
5. *True,* ♡1074 is an ideal holding.
6. *True,* spades were not supported by South, suggesting partner has length and (probably) strength there.

Four out of six is more than enough to be leading a trump – even with three statements 'true' you should be fingering one!

3. A spade
You have a straight choice between two unbid suits and in this circumstance there is little to guide us. However, your only, somewhat fragile, clue is that bidding tends to be oriented towards finding major suit fits – because game in a major only requires ten tricks. In sequences where a major goes 'missing', as with spades here, it almost certainly means neither opponent has four cards in the suit.

Thus your fourth card is highly likely to come into its own. If you lead a club, you might easily be right, but the above analysis is important to bear in mind, nevertheless.

4. A heart
Here we have a simple choice – the surprise of leading our suit or the predictable attack of leading partner's. Many would prefer the latter and, if my heart suit were weaker, so would I. However, many years of leading partner's suit in this kind of position has pushed me into being a gambler.

One does need a certain amount of courage and a supportive partner, to risk leading a heart. If you select 'partner's suit' when another lead would have defeated the contract, it is easily understood and accepted by everyone.

What seems to be less readily accepted is vice-versa. The male bridge player in particular often feels his 'authority' and skill has been called into question when his partner dares to try something else.

Nevertheless, and despite all the foregoing, my experience is that opponents are nearly always prepared for the (predictable) lead of any suit bid against them. Not that it means it will never be right to follow that course. Far from it. One should normally try to find your side's strongest suit and that should be one that you have bid. When there is a good alternative, though, the time may be right to spring a surprise. I leave it to you to decide if your partner is one who can readily accept when this goes wrong! As you can judge, mine have to.

5. A diamond

Listen to the bidding! That is the first rule of defence and here we have a golden opportunity to put that listening to good use.

When the opposition bid and supported diamonds, they showed at least eight between them. We have four, leaving partner with at most one. We can plan our strategy *before* we lead.

Start with a diamond, win ♡A when trumps are played and continue diamonds, giving partner a ruff. A spade is returned to our ace (see how we ensure this in *Winning Bridge at Home*) and we give our partner another ruff. Four tricks in the bank and maybe more if East has anything good to contribute. This is the type of layout we envisage:

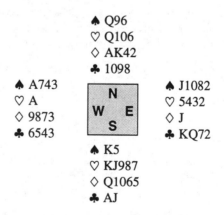

On any other lead, the diamond ruffs would be lost and 4♠ would make quite easily. Congratulations if you worked that one out.

6. A diamond

Normally, we dream of having an 'easy' lead, i.e. one which combines the security of not giving away a trick and attacks a potential enemy weak-spot. A heart appears to be such a lead, and in normal circumstances I would not hesitate in recommending it over a highly risky diamond lead. But these are not normal circumstances.

The bidding has highlighted a need to 'get rich quick'. Dummy's clubs are over our queen, so a finesse will be 'on-side' for declarer and the suit will divide painlessly. If that were not enough, the trumps are in the wrong place (partner's hand) for the defence and all in all we face a depressing picture. Our only hope is to set up our tricks immediately:

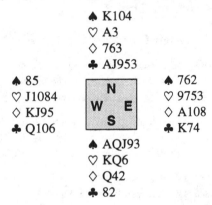

```
                 ♠ K104
                 ♡ A3
                 ◇ 763
                 ♣ AJ953
   ♠ 85             N          ♠ 762
   ♡ J1084                     ♡ 9753
   ◇ KJ95      W      E        ◇ A108
   ♣ Q106          S           ♣ K74
                 ♠ AQJ93
                 ♡ KQ6
                 ◇ Q42
                 ♣ 82
```

Note that when the bidding suggests our cards lie badly for declarer (as in 2 earlier) a passive lead is favoured but, where we see a need for urgency, our most active choice is necessary.

An active lead is usually categorised as one which seeks a quick reward and thus it tends to be either:

(a) a suit with a preponderance of high cards (as here) or
(b) a short suit, often including an honour (such as Ax, Kx, or Qx).

The higher the contract or the more confidently bid, the more an active lead should be paramount in our thoughts.

Summary of Advice on Opening Leads
1. Lead a suit bid by partner unless you have a *clearly* good alternative e.g. QJ109, KQJ, etc.
2. Lead the 'unbid' suit in preference to a suit bid by the opponents.

3. Avoid leading unsupported aces in suit contracts, unless holding great length or against a high level contract.

4. Avoid leading a suit bid by declarer.

5. Lead more passively against lower level contracts, or where you know that your cards are badly placed for declarer. Make active leads when you need to win tricks quickly.

6. Lead your longest suit in no trumps if you have no other clues and lead the strongest of suits with equal length.

7. Prefer a lead 'through' dummy to a lead 'up to' declarer.

> *AND REMEMBER* – Always carefully review the bidding and develop the habit of picturing the opposing cards, *BEFORE YOU LEAD.*

Which Card do We Lead?

You have studied long and hard and come up with the suit to lead, but which *card* do you select? I said at the beginning of this section our lead must tell partner something about the nature of the suit we have chosen. Why is this?

It may be crucial to your chances that partner understands the motives behind your choice of lead, otherwise he may fail to act in the way you wish. How do you differentiate between:

1. When you are trying to get a ruff.
2. When you are trying to establish tricks.
3. When you are trying to find partner's suit.
4. When you have a strong suit of your own?

The simple answer is that you need a code that will enable your partnership to judge the likely holding, both length and strength, in the suit led. It works as follows:

Length of Suit	Card to Lead	
	With an Honour	Without Honours
2 Cards	Top	Top
3 Cards	Lowest	Top
4 Cards	Lowest	Top
5 Cards	4th highest	Top
6 Cards or more	4th highest	Top

In addition to the table, when we possess two or more honours, the card varies with the exact holding:

AK	–	Ace
AQ*	–	Low from 4 or more cards, otherwise ace
AJ*	–	Low from 4 or more cards, otherwise ace
KQ	–	King
KJ	–	Low from 3 or more cards, otherwise king
QJ	–	Queen
J10	–	Jack
109	–	Ten

* Do not lead low from an ace against a suit contract.

That all seems a great deal to absorb in one go, so here are ten suits to familiarise yourself with the basic concept. Which card to you select if leading from the following:

(a) K1043

(b) K10432

(c) QJ97

(d) A10

(e) KJ1082

(f) KQJ4

(g) 7653

(h) 92

(i) Q109

(j) AKJ43

Answers

(a) 3   4th highest from an honour

(b) 3   4th highest, even though you have five cards

(c) Q   From QJ

(d) A   Because you have only 2. Even with 3 or 4, in a trump contract, I would still lead the ace normally, but in no trumps it is better to lead low.

(e) J   KJ10, is treated like J10. You will hear this type of holding referred to as an *interior sequence* – which is not alluding to the colour scheme for the front room. Other such interiors are AJ10, A109, K109, Q109.

(f) K   The possession of the queen *and* jack simply strengthens the suit, it does not change the card.

(g) 7   'Top of nothing' and it really is nothing. A high card such as this is designed to let your partner know you have no interest in the suit. You are leading this suit for 'passive' reasons or to find *partner's* best suit.

(h) 9   Top from a doubleton (always).

(i) 10   Interior sequence, see (e)

(j) A   With a suit as strong as this, it would be rare indeed to advocate leading a low card. Better to shoot from the hip!!

So, the card chosen gives a message about the intent behind leading a particular suit. Armed with that information, the partnership should be nearer to answering one of the key questions about defence: 'Should I switch the attack or continue playing the suit led?' That is our next port of call, but just before we leave card selection, here are a few layouts which should reinforce 'why' the above is the best approach:

(a)   1072

KQJ43   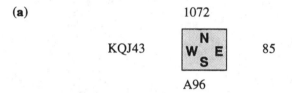   85

A96

Lead the king, otherwise a low card will allow declarer a cheap trick.

(b)   Q84

KJ109   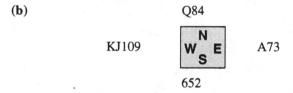   A73

652

Lead the jack, trapping dummy's queen. Partner will retain the ace and the defence will collect 4 tricks from the suit

(c)   654

Q3   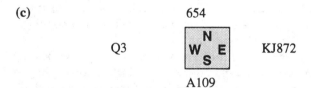   KJ872

A109

Lead the queen, to enable the suit to be unblocked. Imagine that you are declarer (East) tackling this suit – you would play the queen first. The principle holds good in defence too.

(d)

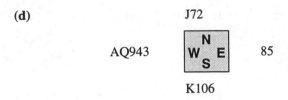

J72

AQ943   85

K106

Lead low, allowing declarer the first trick in the suit. When partner gets in, he leads through declarer's king and you take 4 tricks. An efficient operation. If you lead the ace first, all the above collapses.

(e)

52

AJ1043   876

KQ9

Lead the jack, a low card will allow declarer an extra trick with the 9.

Switching the Defence

If the opening lead is the single greatest cause of allowing bad contracts to make, decisions early on in the play certainly come a close second. In particular, when the defence *next get in* is critical, because declarer is already well on his way. If the lead was accurate, we must continue playing the suit, but if it was off-track, this is liable to be our last chance to find a killing switch.

Here is a defensive problem. Let's see how our thought processes should run:

Dealer South. Love All.

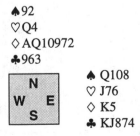

♠ 92
♡ Q4
◇ AQ10972
♣ 963

♠ Q108
♡ J76
◇ K5
♣ KJ874

West	North	East	South
–	–	–	1♡
Pass	2♢	Pass	2NT
Pass	3NT	Pass	Pass
Pass			

Contract 3NT by South. Lead of ♠4.

Partner leads a low spade, which goes to our queen and declarer's king. At trick two, ♢J is played from South, West and North follow and we win our king. Do we play a spade, a heart or a club?

Let us start by eliminating the 'Screaming Lord Sutch' candidate. A heart is foolish because it is declarer's main suit and offers no chance of a quick reward. Remember, we can see lots of diamond winners in dummy and, if declarer has ♡AK as the bidding suggests, then he will make his contract as soon as he gets in. For the defence, it's now or never!

We are down to spades or clubs and we must ask ourselves, 'Can the suit I am leading provide us with enough tricks to beat the contract?' Partner led ♠4; could he still have enough cards left to take four more tricks in the suit?

The answer is 'yes', he would lead the '4' (fourth highest, remember) from AJ743. Hence, spades offer a realistic hope of defeating the contract. You should *return* ♠10. (You play back the highest card if you have only two left, and the lowest from three – so if you held originally ♠Q1083, you would return the ♠3.)

Now, let me change the opening lead to ♠3. An almost insignificant difference, except that partner has shown us exactly four cards in the suit. He has only three left, and even if they are all winners, returning a spade will not beat 3NT. We switch to ♣7 (fourth highest from an honour as before) and hope that West has some good clubs, for example:

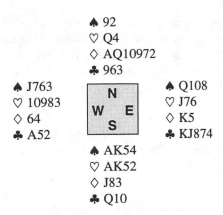

♠ 92
♥ Q4
♦ AQ10972
♣ 963

♠ J763   ♠ Q108
♥ 10983   ♥ J76
♦ 64   ♦ K5
♣ A52   ♣ KJ874

♠ AK54
♥ AK52
♦ J83
♣ Q10

A club switch won by partner's ace, and a club continuation, will earn the defence six tricks (five clubs and a diamond) whereas another spade will leave declarer looking happy.

If West had held a good spade suit, what would have happened?

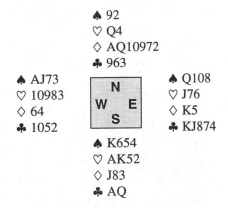

♠ 92
♥ Q4
♦ AQ10972
♣ 963

♠ AJ73   ♠ Q108
♥ 10983   ♥ J76
♦ 64   ♦ K5
♣ 1052   ♣ KJ874

♠ K654
♥ AK52
♦ J83
♣ AQ

True a spade would enable East/West to win four tricks, rather than three (at most) on a club switch, but over-tricks will not make you rich! To win at bridge, you must always beat contracts whenever possible. Even if you 'invest' the odd extra trick in trying, you will still be well ahead in the long run.

Finally, if West had begun with ♠7, what would we have concluded? Could partner have ace, jack to five in the suit, or is it the top of nothing? Just take a moment to see if you can deduce the answer.

To find out the meaning of ♠7, we look at the number of cards outstanding that are higher than it. We can account for the king in declarer's hand, we held Q108, and the 9 in dummy. That leaves only the ace and jack that are higher than partner's lead. The seven could, at best, be his *third* highest, hence we can deduce it is 'top of nothing'. Time to switch, because declarer has ♠AKJ.

Note how important it is to stick rigidly to the method you agree because, had you fancied leading third highest 'for a change', the effect would have been disastrous. It is absolutely essential not to mislead partner, you are in it together.

Here is another 'do you switch or not?' problem:

Dealer South. Game All.

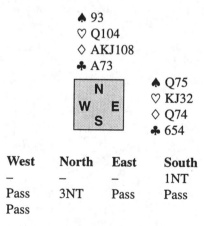

♠ 93
♡ Q104
◇ AKJ108
♣ A73

♠ Q75
♡ KJ32
◇ Q74
♣ 654

West	North	East	South
–	–	–	1NT
Pass	3NT	Pass	Pass
Pass			

Contract 3NT by South. Opening lead of ♠4.

Partner's spade lead goes to your queen and declarer's ace. At trick two, declarer finesses in diamonds, you win your queen and...? Whilst it is certainly true that partner may have ♠K J 8 4 2 when a spade continuation is necessary, there is a subtle reason why it is most unlikely.

The answer lies in declarer's play and I must emphasise here that a defender should always examine the line adopted by declarer. He, after all, can immediately see all his assets, and is less liable to go wrong in the early play – he should be trusted in general.

If we return a spade, we are playing for this layout of the suit:

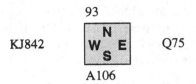

93

KJ842   Q75

A106

Is that reasonable, or has declarer made a faulty play? The answer, as I am sure you suspect, is the latter, because in this situation declarer could 'hold-up' his ace, thus preventing us from ever reaching partner, for example:

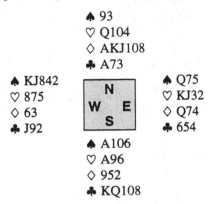

♠ 93
♡ Q104
◊ AKJ108
♣ A73

♠ KJ842   ♠ Q75
♡ 875   ♡ KJ32
◊ 63   ◊ Q74
♣ J92   ♣ 654

♠ A106
♡ A96
◊ 952
♣ KQ108

The contract is completely safe provided declarer ducks the first two rounds of spades and wins the third. Now when we gain the lead, as East, with ◊Q, we have no more spades to play, and South can take his tricks in peace and quiet.

So, if we can eliminate that position, is there an alternative approach which might succeed? Consider this:

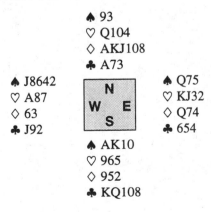

♠ 93
♡ Q104
◊ AKJ108
♣ A73

♠ J8642   ♠ Q75
♡ A87   ♡ KJ32
◊ 63   ◊ Q74
♣ J92   ♣ 654

♠ AK10
♡ 965
◊ 952
♣ KQ108

A heart switch, whilst appearing almost suicidal in comparison to a spade return, does in fact get the job done. Of course, if West does not hold ♡A, we will look a little silly, as dummy collects an easy trick, but we will have tried our best to beat the contract.

So remember, the art of good defence is to 'read the table' and that includes:

1. Inferences from partner's opening lead.
2. Inferences from the bidding.
3. Inferences from declarer's line of play.

4
GENERAL PRINCIPLES OF DEFENSIVE PLAY

To date I have concentrated on the early moves of the defence and, in truth, they are by a long way the most vital. However, it is still important to have an awareness of good technique at all times, and this section will deal with some of the basic 'dos' and don'ts'.

Third Hand High

This phrase is as old as the hills, maybe even older, and owes it origin, I believe, to whist. While it is generally true, I must stress there are many exceptions to this rule. But, before I assassinate it, I will at least show you some examples of it performing well.

Play high when partner leads a low card (indicating an honour) and dummy has small cards, for example:

♠ 62

♠ AJ753

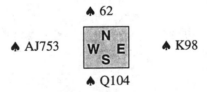

♠ K98

♠ Q104

West leads ♠5 against a no trump contract and East must rise with his highest card – in this example, preventing South from making an unnecessary trick in the suit.

♠ 62

♠ KJ753

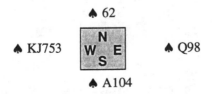

♠ Q98

♠ A104

Playing ♠Q prevents South from winning the 10. Or:

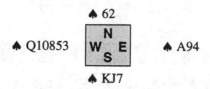

Winning ♠A and returning the suit holds declarer to one trick in the suit.

The idea behind all these plays is that East is attempting to win the trick himself but, if he cannot do so, he will at least dislodge a high card from declarer's hand. That will hopefully promote West's honours into tricks. Here is a final example of 'third hand high':

West leads the jack (an interior sequence) against no trumps, and East must play the king or allow South to break out into a big grin.

Play high when dummy has a higher card than your highest, but follows low, for example:

West leads ♠2 (fourth best) against a trump contract and dummy plays low. East should play his highest card in this situation – I will allow you to follow through the developments in the suit.

Again, the ♠2 is lead and East must play his jack or invite the wrath of West and the scorn of South.

Before we move onto where we need to modify third hand high, a brief word about how to deal with two or more honours:

♠ 854

♠ K962   ♠ QJ7

♠ A103

Again West chooses the ♠2. Do we, as East, play the queen or the jack? If we were leading this suit, the queen would be our choice, showing that we possess the jack as well, so do we follow that rule here? I am afraid we do not.

The reason is that if we play the queen, partner cannot tell if we hold the jack because we are forced to play the queen from many other holdings e.g. ♠Q73. However, if we choose the lowest honour of our sequence (in this case the jack), declarer will still be obliged to win with the *ace*.

West will realise immediately that we hold the queen, because declarer would have won the trick with the queen if he had it! Hence, playing an honour in the third seat, denies the touching honour below it.

Finessing against Dummy

When we declare contracts and take finesses, we have about a 50/50 chance of success, although it can seem a great deal lower than that. In defence, we can improve significantly on those odds, because we can take finesses knowing where the key card is placed. Let me return to a suit I gave you earlier:

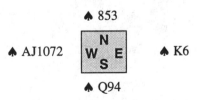

♠ 853

♠ AJ1072   ♠ K6

♠ Q94

When West led the jack, East put up the king to ensure South did not win a silly trick with the queen.

Now consider this:

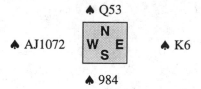

♠ Q53

♠ AJ1072   ♠ K6

♠ 984

Again, the jack is led, but this time East can see the queen in dummy, so there is no need to waste the king (unless declarer covers the opening lead). In effect, the defence has nullified the queen whether it is in dummy or in declarer's hand. They have finessed with a 100% success rate. Here are some other examples which could be categorised under the heading *finessing against dummy*.

As East, which card do you play on the first round of spades (in all cases, declarer is in a no trump contract, and dummy follows low)?

(a)

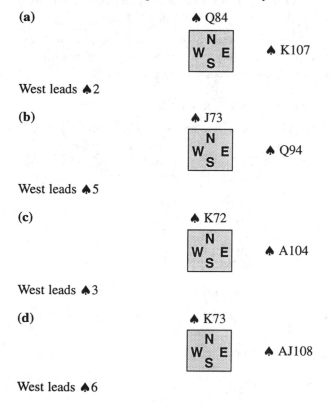

♠ Q84

♠ K107

West leads ♠2

(b)

♠ J73

♠ Q94

West leads ♠5

(c)

♠ K72

♠ A104

West leads ♠3

(d)

♠ K73

♠ AJ108

West leads ♠6

(e)

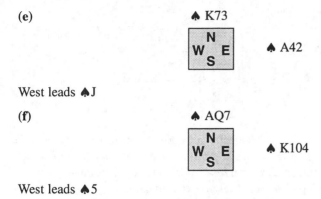

♠ K73

♠ A42

West leads ♠J

(f)

♠ AQ7

♠ K104

West leads ♠5

Answers

(a) Play ♠10, hoping for a layout such as:

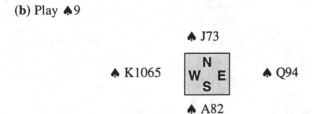

♠ Q84

♠ AJ32

♠ K107

♠ 965

The 10 will hold the trick and you continue with the king and a third round to partner who can cash the thirteenth. If you rise with the king at trick one, the queen cannot be denied her day.

(b) Play ♠9

♠ J73

♠ K1065

♠ Q94

♠ A82

The 9 will force the ace and the jack will be nullified. If you are confused by these plays, just imagine yourself to be East, declaring a contract and playing spades. You would normally have to guess the location of ♠J, but if you knew North held the card, you would play a low spade to the nine and take three tricks. Same thing.

(c) Play ♠10.

♠ K72

♠ J963   ♠ A104

♠ Q85

If we rise with the ace, we will allow the king and queen to take tricks independently. However, if we insert the 10, West can later lead ♠J through dummy and the king will lose his crown. Again, think of how you would tackle the East/West cards if you were declarer:

♠ A104

♠ J963

You would finesse twice, hoping that each defender started with one of the missing honours.

(d) Play ♠10

♠ K73

♠ 654   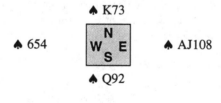   ♠ AJ108

♠ Q92

(e) Play ♠2

♠ K73

♠ J1095      ♠ A42

♠ Q86

These problems are quite similar in that the opponents have the king and queen of the suit, and the defence are trying to ensure that they only win one trick. In each case, East must make sure that the ace is reserved for taking dummy's honour, and not being wasted on 'thin air'.

(f) Play ♠10.

♠ AQ7
♠ J965   ♠ K104
♠ 832

Just because declarer played low in dummy, do not draw the conclusion that there is an honour in the suit. It is quite feasible that South prefers to leave the finesse until later, or simply wishes East to be on lead with this suit protected from further attack. Do not play the king, therefore, imagining that South must have the jack. Had West led a higher card, such as ♠9 (top of nothing), East could be sure that declarer held ♠J.

Before we leave 'finessing against dummy', a word of caution. Sometimes we are faced with a tricky choice and we get it wrong. Let's return to problem (b) and you'll see what I mean:

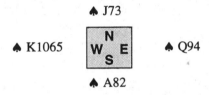

♠ J73
♠ K1065   ♠ Q94
♠ A82

I advocated the 9, to finesse against dummy's jack. However, assuming we are still defending a no trump contract, this might also be the layout:

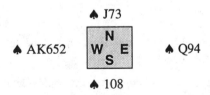

♠ J73
♠ AK652   ♠ Q94
♠ 108

West, with no outside entry, may elect to duck a round of spades, and lead ♠5 rather than the ace, playing for this type of situation:

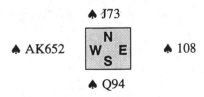

♠ J73
♠ AK652   ♠ 108
♠ Q94

After South wins the first trick, East can still reach partner's suit. If West cashes even one top card, the opportunity to establish the suit has gone.

If we play ♠9 from ♠Q94, and partner does indeed have the ♠AK, we will look mighty silly. Nevertheless, this should not deter us. Why? Because there are *three* holdings West might have, where playing the 9 is necessary:

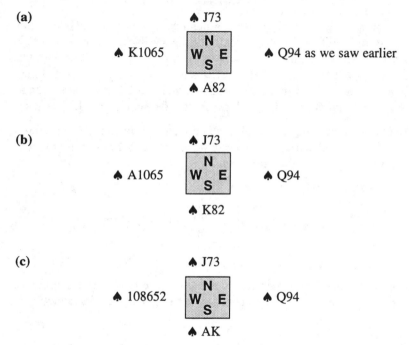

(a) ♠ J73 / ♠ K1065 (W) / ♠ A82 (S) / ♠ Q94 (E) as we saw earlier

(b) ♠ J73 / ♠ A1065 (W) / ♠ K82 (S) / ♠ Q94 (E)

(c) ♠ J73 / ♠ 108652 (W) / ♠ AK (S) / ♠ Q94 (E)

3 to 1 is pretty good odds, but don't blame me if the first time you make such a play it was the 'one'!

To summarise, our rules for playing in third chair relate to how we react to our partner's lead. We are attempting to work out:

1. What partner's intentions are.
2. How best to help.

Second Hand Low

We need to know how best to respond to a variety of different situations in order to get the best out of our often meagre resources. To go with third hand high is second hand low. Hardly Shakespearean, but at least you can remember it.

This example will show us the basic idea:

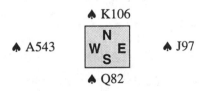

Here is how the spade suit is divided round the table. Assume to begin with that the lead is South's. If the ♠2 is played and West rushes in with the ace, South will take an easy two tricks. If West plays 'second hand low', South will win only one trick.

Further if East led ♠7, and South rose with the queen immediately, East would get a 'free' second winner from the suit. Same principle.

Additionally, we must always endeavour to make life hard for declarer, and never save him or her a guess, for example:

Declarer, South, leads a card and West, correctly, plays small. The jack is tried from North and East scoops the trick. Should South at a later date continue this suit, West must play low *again*. It is more than likely that another losing finesse will be taken and a third trick obtained. More tricks are lost through taking aces too quickly, than by holding on to them too long.

Unless you leave declarer to guess the lie of the cards, you will give up the only real advantage the defenders have.

For many years I have seen this scenario recur. South leads ♠4 and West deems it necessary to play the queen. Such phrases follow as:

'I was forcing out the ace, partner.'
'I had to play it then, or lose it.'
'It was there for him, anyway.'

All West has done is to make declarer's life as easy as can be. Far from achieving anything positive, the only effect has been to solve a guess in the suit. Instead of a 50% chance of winning a trick, West now has zero. The only point in second hand playing high is, as you will see, to cover an honour. Otherwise play low, even in the most strange situations, e.g:

South needs to develop this suit and for reasons best known to himself (maybe a shortage of entries to dummy) starts by leading low from hand. It is difficult for West to follow smoothly with the '2', but it is neverthe-less the correct play.

Declarer will probably insert the 10 and lose to East's jack. The next lead will usually come from North (the queen) and a finesse will be taken through East's 'known' king. West will produce 'the card he shouldn't have', and the defence will secure a second trick. But how can you be sure that it is safe to play low? Couldn't this be the layout?

Now ducking on the first round will leave egg on poor old West's face, because declarer will continue with a low card to the ace, dropping the king. West will have lost a 'certain' trick.

The answer to my question lies in looking at those North/South cards again. Who would tackle the suit by leading low from the South hand, if they had that combined holding? Everyone would cross to North, and lead an honour, intending to finesse against East. Therefore, as West, you are perfectly safe to duck should declarer lead low from his hand, but do it *smoothly*. If you think too long, you give the game away.

Covering an Honour

You should know by now there is always an exception to any rule and second hand low is no different. Consider this layout:

♠ AJ9865

♠ K3   ♠ 1074

♠ Q2

South leads ♠Q and West, who has only read the first part of this chapter, plays low. The queen wins the trick of course, and now another spade is lead to the king and ace. Finally, dummy's ♠J captures East's 10. East/West have nothing to show for their efforts. How could they do better?

As you will have appreciated, I am sure, West must 'cover' South's queen with the king, forcing out the ace from dummy. Now after cashing ♠J, North must concede a trick to East. In effect, West's king has gone down fighting, taking both the queen and ace to neutralise him. Here is another position:

♠ AJ98

♠ K65   ♠ 1043

♠ Q72

If South leads ♠2 towards dummy, West must play a low card. However, if South tries ♠Q first, West must be alert and cover with the king, to eventually promote partner's ten in the way we saw earlier.

A pattern is beginning to emerge, which could be summarised by *'Cover an honour with an honour'*. How low is an honour? What about the '10'?

♠ AJ973

♠ K2   ♠ Q865

♠ 104

If South leads ♠10, West must use the king to drive out dummy's ace. Now East will come to two tricks in the suit – the modest ♠8 being promoted to a winner. So we can count the 10 as an honour. And the 9?

♠ AJ1073

♠ K2   ♠ Q865

♠ 94

When ♠9 is led, West is in the same position as above, needing to play the king to gain a second trick for the defence. But again note that, if South leads ♠4, West must play low. The art of covering honours is to take two of theirs for one of yours. In that way all the intermediate cards in your partner's hand move one rung up the ladder.

Sometimes, we cannot see the 'key' holding in a suit, for example:

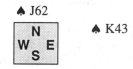

♠ J62

♠ K43

We are East, defending a contract and dummy leads ♠J. We do not know South's holding, so we must fall back on our principles of covering the honour.

♠ J62

♠ 1085   ♠ K43

♠ AQ97

Again, we have unselfishly created a winner in partner's hand.

Consecutive (or Touching) Honours

When we see two or more consecutive or touching honours in dummy, we must slightly adapt our rule for when to cover. See if you can work out why by looking at this example:

Suppose that ♠J is led from North. On the theory of covering honours, East should play the queen. However, South will win the ace and return the suit. Whilst West can now gather the king, dummy's 10 will take care of the remaining cards. North/South will have managed the suit for one loser.

That could not be said to be a great achievement for East/West, as West's king was a certain winner from the outset. Can they do better?

We must go back to East's decision to cover ♠J. Suppose that East plays low instead. West will gather the trick with the king, of course. These are the cards that remain:

When North next gains the lead, and plays ♠10, East should now cover with the queen, thereby promoting his partner's nine into a second trick.

Hence, using this example, we must add one major exception to our rule of covering honours with honours, as follows:

> '*When there are consecutive honours in dummy, always cover the last one played.*'

Try this:

South is declarer, you are East and dummy leads ♠Q do you play the king or a low card? The answer is 'low' because of this possible layout:

♠ QJ4

♠ 1065   ♠ K73

♠ A982

If the first trick goes Q, K, A, 5, South can continue with ♠9 and finesse against West's 10. If we follow low on the queen (and later cover the jack if led), South is denied the chance to smother West's trick.

Quiz

Before we move on to the final chapter on defence, 'Signals and Discards', here are a few examples to try out for yourself. In all cases, declarer is South. In questions 1, 2 and 3 which card do you play as West? In questions 4 and 5, which card do you play as East?

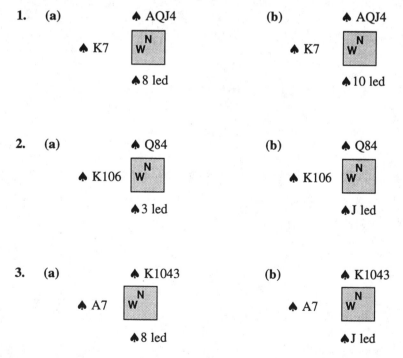

1.   (a)   ♠ AQJ4   (b)   ♠ AQJ4

      ♠ K7   ♠ K7

                    ♠8 led   ♠10 led

2.   (a)   ♠ Q84   (b)   ♠ Q84

      ♠ K106   ♠ K106

                    ♠3 led   ♠J led

3.   (a)   ♠ K1043   (b)   ♠ K1043

      ♠ A7   ♠ A7

                    ♠8 led   ♠J led

4. (a)   ♠ Q104   (b) ♠ Q104

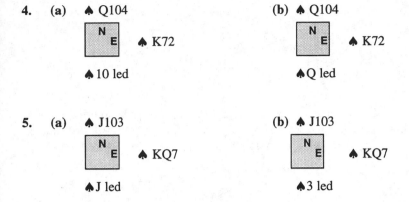

5. (a)   ♠ J103   (b) ♠ J103

Answers

1. (a) ♠7. No point in 'wasting' the king on fresh air. Make declarer work hard to pick up the suit, and don't let him know where the enemy cards are.

   (b) ♠K. Cover the 10, in case this is the layout:

                        ♠ AQJ4

   ♠ K7   W N E   ♠ 96532
                 S

                        ♠ 108

Now East's 9 will come into its own.

2.   (a)   ♠6. Although the king appears to be the natural play, it must be resisted. This may be how the suit is divided:

                        ♠ Q84

   ♠ K106   W N E   ♠ A92
                 S

                        ♠ J753

By playing the king without taking an honour with it you will leave South with two tricks in the suit. Even if declarer has the ace, there is no hurry to win your trick.

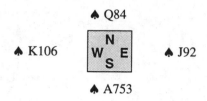

Due to the fortunate layout, North/South will always be entitled to three tricks in spades and East/West only one. The overall result will not be affected if West wins the first, second or third round of the suit.

(b) ♠K. In case South is being crafty!

Failure to rise with the king will eventually result in the queen being promoted. Remember, it is OK to cover an honour in second position.

3. (a) ♠7. We are not sure what South holds, but it is of no benefit to us to go charging in, for example:

South might have been planning to run the ♠8 through West, hoping he held the jack. As soon as we rise unmajestically, the game is up.

(b) ♠A. To cater for anything similar to the following:

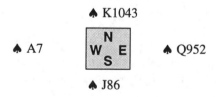

The rule of covering honours applies just as much to the ace as any other card. Here East/West will win three tricks after West plays ♠A, two otherwise.

4. (a) ♠2. Do not be tempted into anything rash when declarer leads a middle honour. You have little to gain and can often lose.

♠ Q104

♠ J53

♠ K72

♠ A986

North leads ♠10, hoping to coax East into covering with an honour. Should East oblige, declarer's reward will be to unravel the suit *at no loss*. After capturing the king, continuing with the ♠9 will nullify West's jack. If East calmly plays low on the ♠10, South will lose a trick.

(b) ♠K. You cannot treat this situation like those with two honours, because the *honours are not consecutive*. Whilst the king is recommended in case partner has the jack, it is quite acceptable to duck the queen, particularly if South bid the suit and partner may, therefore, have a bare ace.

♠ Q104

♠ A

♠ K72

♠ J98653

However, having elected to duck, you must not cover the 10 if it is led from dummy next, in case of:

♠ Q104

♠ J3

♠ K72

♠ A9865

So there are really two correct answers, the ♠K initially or ♠2 *followed by* ♠7 next round.

5. (a) ♠Q. When you have two honours and dummy has a further two, we go back to covering an honour with an honour. Sorry if this seems too much to absorb in one go, but it's all worth it, believe me!

♠ J103

♠ 942

♠ KQ7

♠ A865

East/West can guarantee themselves two tricks with accurate play, or one trick with inaccurate play!

(b) ♠7. Refer to the layout above to confirm this, but note for the future that one should not instinctively play high cards in second seat, more the reverse. *If in doubt, keep down* (not very good, I know, but I was struggling for a catchy phrase).

5
SIGNALS AND DISCARDS

Signals

We start with a question: 'What is the purpose of a signal?'

In essence, the answer is: *'It enables defenders to co-operate fully'*. This is achieved by allowing them to 'say' whether they like the direction of the defence their partner is following. So, if I am defending with you and you lead a particular suit, my 'signal' will tell you whether you have struck gold or struck out. I can play a card which will encourage you to continue this attack or change tack.

Before we get involved in the signalling mechanism itself, let me first scotch one myth. Many players say that they do not like giving signals, 'because it only helps declarer place the cards'. Whilst this is certainly true from time to time, it is nevertheless an unsound argument. Nine times out of ten (at least), the defence has a greater and more urgent need to know where its assets are, and effective signals are one of the few ways that this can be accomplished. So don't be persuaded by the 'head in the sand' group: the earth is not flat!

The simplest signal would be to smile if partner does something you like and frown when he doesn't. Unfortunately, that option is not available to us or you could skip the next few pages.

Here is a basic situation, you are East deciding what to play:

Dealer South. Game All.

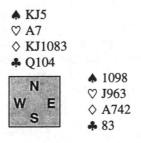

```
              ♠ KJ5
              ♡ A7
              ◇ KJ1083
              ♣ Q104
                              ♠ 1098
                   N          ♡ J963
              W         E     ◇ A742
                   S          ♣ 83
```

West	North	East	South
–	–	–	1♠
Pass	2◇	Pass	2♠
Pass	4♠	Pass	Pass
Pass			

Partner leads ♣A, suggesting possession of the king, dummy plays the four and you have to decide how to play. You would like to tell West that you like clubs continued, because you can ruff the third round. The standard way to do that, although there is no technical reason why it is so, is to play a high card to encourage (come on) and a low card to discourage (go away).

Just remember: **H**igh **E**ncouraging **L**ow **D**iscouraging (H E L D)

In our example you would play ♣8 encouraging West to continue his attack. You are hoping for a layout such as this:

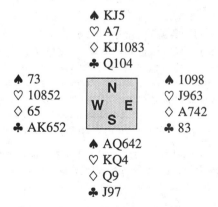

```
                    ♠ KJ5
                    ♡ A7
                    ◇ KJ1083
                    ♣ Q104
        ♠ 73                        ♠ 1098
        ♡ 10852      N              ♡ J963
        ◇ 65      W     E           ◇ A742
        ♣ AK652      S              ♣ 83
                    ♠ AQ642
                    ♡ KQ4
                    ◇ Q9
                    ♣ J97
```

West continues with ♣K at trick two and another club at trick three giving you the much-needed ruff. Your ◇A is the vital fourth trick for the defence.

The ♣8 is not encouraging per se, it is the fact that it was *higher than another card* you held in the suit. So when you followed on the second round with ♣3, West *then* knew that you wanted the suit continued. Contrast that with this example:

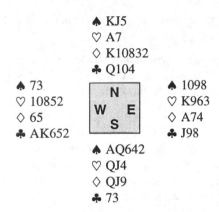

```
              ♠ KJ5
              ♡ A7
              ◇ K10832
              ♣ Q104
♠ 73                          ♠ 1098
♡ 10852          N            ♡ K963
◇ 65         W       E        ◇ A74
♣ AK652          S            ♣ J98
              ♠ AQ642
              ♡ QJ4
              ◇ QJ9
              ♣ 73
```

On the ♣A, East still follows with ♣8, except now it is discouraging – East wants West to switch to hearts. However, West is unaware of the meaning of partner's card to begin with, and continues with ♣K to cater for our first example.

This time, though, East follows with the ♣9 on the second round, so West knows that partner did not like the suit (otherwise East would have played ♣9 first). West must now switch to hearts.

Please note that a signal does not necessarily relate to the length in the suit. We have seen that we can discourage with three cards; here is the other side of the coin.

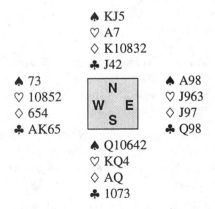

```
              ♠ KJ5
              ♡ A7
              ◇ K10832
              ♣ J42
♠ 73                          ♠ A98
♡ 10852          N            ♡ J963
◇ 654        W       E        ◇ J97
♣ AK65           S            ♣ Q98
              ♠ Q10642
              ♡ KQ4
              ◇ AQ
              ♣ 1073
```

Again, the contract is 4♠ by South, and West leads ♣A. If East mistakenly plays ♣8, the consequences will be disastrous. Sure, West will continue with clubs, because the 8 is liable to be a 'come-on' signal, but when he sees the 9 on the second trick, he will conclude that East really never wanted clubs at all.

The probable heart switch will then allow declarer to pitch a club loser and make the contract. To avoid this calamity, East must begin with ♣9, then his partner will play a third round as desired.

Discards

We have looked briefly at signals and how they assist defenders. The other major tool available to us is a system of discards. We can then have a method of putting over our views on a hand, whether we follow suit or not. We are no longer the 'one-armed man'.

The 'standard' approach to discarding mirrors that of signalling, in that a high card is encouraging and a low one discouraging. Whilst having on its side the element of simplicity, there are nevertheless severe drawbacks, for example:

Dealer North. Game All.

♠ Q4
♡ 652
◇ AKJ103
♣ 765

♠ J9653
♡ 1097
◇ 2
♣ AJ93

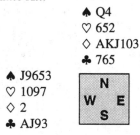

West	North	East	South
–	Pass	Pass	1◇
Pass	3◇	Pass	3NT
Pass	Pass	Pass	

You are West, defending against South's 3NT contract. You begin with the normal lead of ♠5 (fourth highest from an honour) which is won in dummy with the queen. Next comes ◇A and ◇K and you have your first discard. What should it be?

To have any chance of beating the contract a club switch is essential, but to discard a high club, in order to get what you need, will necessitate you throwing a winner away! Then, even with a club switch, you will win only four tricks(a hoped for ◇Q and, three clubs). It is essential to devise a method of discarding which can put over the required message, without costing you a trick in doing so. Standard discards clearly won't do.

The best way to achieve our objective is always to throw a suit you do not want, or *discard 'rubbish'*. Partner can eliminate that suit from enquiries, regardless of the size of the card thrown. In the example, West throws a spade first and then ♡7. Partner should then switch to clubs. Even though ♡7 may superficially be a 'high' card, and hence appear to be encouraging, East knows that this is a suit in which partner holds rubbish, and can ignore the size of the card played. This was the actual hand:

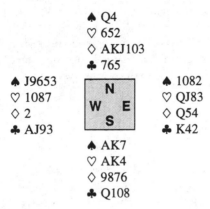

```
                    ♠ Q4
                    ♡ 652
                    ◇ AKJ103
                    ♣ 765
  ♠ J9653            N          ♠ 1082
  ♡ 1087                        ♡ QJ83
  ◇ 2         W          E      ◇ Q54
  ♣ AJ93            S          ♣ K42
                    ♠ AK7
                    ♡ AK4
                    ◇ 9876
                    ♣ Q108
```

Here is another example:

Dealer East. North/South Game.

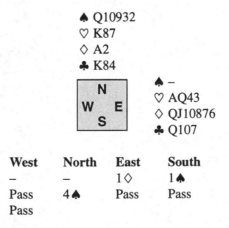

```
                    ♠ Q10932
                    ♡ K87
                    ◇ A2
                    ♣ K84
                     N          ♠ —
                                ♡ AQ43
               W          E     ◇ QJ10876
                     S          ♣ Q107
```

West	North	East	South
–	–	1◇	1♠
Pass	4♠	Pass	Pass
Pass			

West leads ◇ K, in response to your opening bid, won in dummy by the ace. Declarer continues with a spade and looks slightly disappointed when you start thinking. What do you discard?

Although you do not wish partner to continue diamonds, it is important not to discard from that suit, because it will not help West decide whether to switch to hearts or clubs. You must make a more positive statement. Discard ♣7.

It is up to West to work out that a diamond continuation serves little purpose (you might also have followed with ◇ 6 at trick one to make the message even clearer), and that it is 'now or never' to lead another suit 'through' dummy. Despite East's club being quite high, West knows that it is the suit partner does *not* want, and should switch to a heart if and when the lead is regained. The defence can then take their heart tricks before declarer has a chance to throw one away.

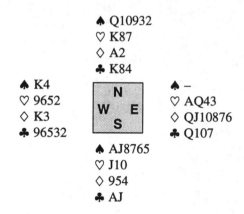

```
                    ♠ Q10932
                    ♡ K87
                    ◇ A2
                    ♣ K84
    ♠ K4          ┌─────────┐      ♠ –
    ♡ 9652        │    N    │      ♡ AQ43
    ◇ K3          │  W   E  │      ◇ QJ10876
    ♣ 96532       │    S    │      ♣ Q107
                  └─────────┘
                    ♠ AJ8765
                    ♡ J10
                    ◇ 954
                    ♣ AJ
```

I will return to discards and signals in *Winning Bridge at Home*, to look at 'suit preference' techniques and other advances.

Quiz

Here is a test on the contents of this chapter.

You are East defending South's 3NT contract, which card would you play in the following examples:

1. (a)

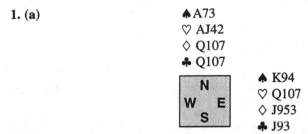

    ♠ A73
    ♡ AJ42
    ◇ Q107
    ♣ Q107
                        ♠ K94
                        ♡ Q107
                        ◇ J953
                        ♣ J93

West leads ♠Q, dummy wins with the ace, and you ...?

   (b) If your spades were ♠K 4, how would you play?

2. (a)

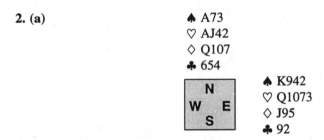

    ♠ A73
    ♡ AJ42
    ◇ Q107
    ♣ 654
                        ♠ K942
                        ♡ Q1073
                        ◇ J95
                        ♣ 92

West leads ♣K, dummy plays low, and you ...?

   (b) If your clubs were ♣J95 which card would you play?
   (c) If your clubs were ♣A2, how would you play?

3. (a)

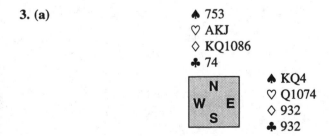

    ♠ 753
    ♡ AKJ
    ◇ KQ1086
    ♣ 74
                        ♠ KQ4
                        ♡ Q1074
                        ◇ 932
                        ♣ 932

Partner leads ♡9, dummy winning the ace, and you ...?

(b) If your hearts were ♡ 10742, which card would you play?

4. (a)

♠ Q107
♡ Q107
◇ K954
♣ A64

♠ J9865
♡ KJ43
◇ 7
♣ 932

Partner leads ♣5 to dummy's ace and you follow with the ♣2. Now comes ◇ K, and another diamond. You discard ...?

(b) In the same situation, what would you throw away from the following hand?

♠ KJ432
♡ J986
◇ 7
♣ 932

Answers

1. (a) ♠9. Encouraging West to continue the suit.

(b) ♠K. To cater for this set up:

♠ A73

♠ QJ1086 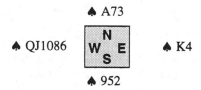 ♠ K4

♠ 952

Now with our king 'unblocked', West can run his winners in the suit.

2. (a) ♣2. Discouraging. Note that if West had led ♣A against a suit contract, you would follow with the 9. Same cards, but you wish to send a different message.

(b) ♣9. Showing a liking for clubs, because of holding ♣J. Partner's lead of ♣K suggests he has the queen, so it is of paramount importance to him to who has the jack.

(c) ♣A. To continue the suit, for example:

♣ 654

♣ KQ1087 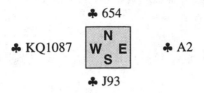 ♣ A2

♣ J93

The defence will take the first five tricks whereas, if East plays ♣2, West will need another entry to run the suit.

Note that with ♣KQ543 or similar it is wise, when defending a no trump contract, to lead a low card at trick one, thus avoiding this embarrassing situation:

♣ 876

♣ KQ543 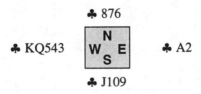 ♣ A2

♣ J109

When East puts the ace on partner's king, it promotes a surprise trick for declarer.

3. (a) ♡7. Although a spade switch may be necessary to defeat the contract, it is a gamble. You *know* that a heart is good for you, so tell partner.

(b) ♡2. Now you need to indicate that partner must not continue with hearts. You hope West will switch to spades rather than clubs, and in *Winning Bridge at Home* we will see how to help West do that.

4. (a) ♠5. Discard from the suit you do not want led. Even though you have five spades and only four hearts, prospects of defeating the contract lie in the heart suit, for example:

♡ Q107

♡ A52 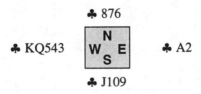 ♡ KJ4 3

♡ 986

Spades offer no such 'quick fix'.

(b) ♡6. It is possible that a heart discard will allow an extra trick in the suit if declarer has four, but it is nonetheless a risk worth taking to ensure that you get a spade lead.

6
HIGH-LEVEL OPENINGS AND RESPONSES

The Two Level

In *Play Bridge at Home* I dealt extensively with opening bids but remained firmly anchored to the ground! Now it is time to look at what higher level openings mean and how we respond to them.

The two level is reserved for very strong hands, rich in playing strength, that will almost certainly play at least a game contract, for example:

♠ AKJ1094
♡ AKQ42
◊ 7
♣ 6

If you are lucky enough to pick up those 13 cards, you would fancy a crack at game, without knowing anything about partner's hand. But how do you ensure that your partner will keep the bidding open? If you choose to open 1♠ and your partner has:

♠ 8
♡ 109653
◊ A432
♣ 987

He will pass your opening bid and you will have the 'joy' of playing 1♠ with a slam available in hearts! How do we get round this problem?

The answer is to have a bid which describes our hand *and forces* partner to respond, regardless of strength. These are *'strong twos'*. So, with our example hand, we open 2♠ saying that we have a great hand with spades as our main suit, *and* forcing partner to respond even holding complete rubbish.

To assist in making sense of partner's reply, we introduce our first convention, *A 2NT response to a two-level opening is a 'negative'*. As such, it implies that the player would have considered passing over a one level opening e.g. up to about six points. Remember 'pass' is not an option over a strong two-level opening, so we have to substitute another bid for it.

If opener rebids his suit over a negative reply, responder can pass at that stage. Otherwise responder must keep the bidding alive, so our example hands might be bid as follows:

Dealer South. Love All.

♠ 8
♡ 109653
◇ A432
♣ 987

♠ AKJ1094
♡ AKQ42
◇ 7
♣ 6

West	North	East	South
–	–	–	2♠
Pass	2NT(i)	Pass	3♡(ii)
Pass	4♡	Pass	Pass
Pass			

(i)   Negative
(ii) Forcing North to bid again, as it is a new suit.

If you are wondering how we reach a slam, that will come later, for now be grateful not to play in 1♠!

If responder has a reasonable hand and a sensible suit, he bids just as over a one-level opening, except that now the sequence is 'forcing to game', i.e. it cannot stop below game level, for example:

Dealer South. Love All.

```
                  ♠ 8
                  ♡ J965
                  ◊ AQJ42
                  ♣ 765
```

```
              N
          W       E
              S
```

```
                  ♠ AKJ10942
                  ♡ AK
                  ◊ 76
                  ♣ K4
```

West	North	East	South
–	–	–	2♠(i)
Pass	3◊(ii)	Pass	3♠(iii)
Pass	4♠(iv)	Pass	Pass
Pass			

(i)   South comfortably has sufficient strength to open at the two-level (usually eight certain tricks, and about 16 points is the lower limit).

(ii) North shows the diamond suit, but nevertheless has a fairly minimum *positive* response.

(iii) Had North responded 2NT, this bid would not be forcing, but South knows that North will continue to game because of the 3◊ bid.

(iv) Despite having only one spade, North must not be lured into bidding 3NT. Once South has rebid his suit, it must be 'self-supporting'. To raise to 4♠ is essential with no stop in an un-bid suit. 3NT would be acceptable with:

```
                  ♠ 8
                  ♡ Q1095
                  ◊ AJ942
                  ♣ QJ6
```

Quiz

Here is a short test to check your understanding of two-level openings and their responses:

1. How many tricks do you need as a minimum to open at the two level?

2. What does a 2NT response mean?

3. Bid these pairs of hands (South is always dealer):

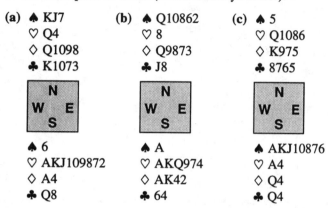

(a) ♠ KJ7
♡ Q4
◇ Q1098
♣ K1073

(b) ♠ Q10862
♡ 8
◇ Q9873
♣ J8

(c) ♠ 5
♡ Q1086
◇ K975
♣ 8765

♠ 6
♡ AKJ109872
◇ A4
♣ Q8

♠ A
♡ AKQ974
◇ AK42
♣ 64

♠ AKJ10876
♡ A4
◇ Q4
♣ Q4

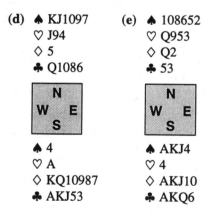

(d) ♠ KJ1097
♡ J94
◇ 5
♣ Q1086

(e) ♠ 108652
♡ Q953
◇ Q2
♣ 53

♠ 4
♡ A
◇ KQ10987
♣ AKJ53

♠ AKJ4
♡ 4
◇ AKJ10
♣ AKQ6

Answers

1. Eight tricks and usually *at least* 16 points, although this type of hand would be an exception:

♠ AKQJ98
♡ AJ1065
◇ 7
♣ 6

2. Less than 7 points (or up to 8 *without* a reasonable suit). A 'negative' reply.

3. (a)

South	North
2♡	3NT(i)
4♡	Pass

(i) With too much for a negative 2NT and no good suit, North describes the hand with a jump to 3NT (about 9-12 points and stops in all suits outside hearts).

(b)

South	North
2♡	2NT
3◇ (i)	5◇ (ii)
Pass	

(i) A new suit, and therefore forcing
(ii) With five card support, North is delighted to jump to game.

(c)

South	North
1♠(i)	Pass

(i) This hand is not quite worth a 2-level opening as there is no guarantee of eight tricks. Further, if partner passes an opening 1♠ bid, there is little fear of missing game. As we can see, 4♠ is hopeless and even 3♠ is no picnic. Had we opened 2♠, this would have been the likely sequence:

South	North
2♠	2NT
3♠(i)	Pass

(i) Not forcing because South repeated the opening suit.

(d)

South	North
2◇	2♠(i)
3♣	4♣
4♡(ii)	5♣
Pass	

(i) Although North has a close decision between 2♠ and a negative 2NT, the strength of the spade suit tips the balance.

(ii) A cuebid trying for a slam in diamonds (see *Winning Bridge at Home*).

(e)

South	North
2♣(i)	2◇(ii)
2♠(iii)	4♠
Pass	

(i) The 2♣ opener is slightly different to the other 2-bids in that it is used to describe those hands of great strength that do not possess an outstanding suit. Here, South does not want to give partner the impression that he is overly strong in any suit, so he commences with a global 'strong' bid of 2♣. Here are some other 2♣ openings:

(a)   ♠ KJ10
       ♡ AK4
       ◇ AK4
       ♣ AQ93

(a) Then follow with 2NT to show a super strong balanced hand (23-24 points). With 25-26 points (if you are ever lucky enough to hold so many) rebid 3NT.

(b)   ♠ 7
       ♡ AQJ4
       ◇ 7
       ♣ AKQJ1086

(b) Follow with 3♣. This is like a '*strong 2 in clubs*'.

(c)   ♠ AKJ4
       ♡ AKQ4
       ◇ AKJ4
       ♣ 4

(c) Follow with 2♡ over 2◇ to leave partner room to show a long suit.

(ii) Rather than use 2NT as a negative, which we do for all the other 2-openings, it makes much more sense to have a '2◊ negative'. This gives the 2♣ opener more space for description, and means that if he is balanced, the weak hand will not be declarer (it is usually better for the opponents to have to 'lead into strength').

(iii) South should not bid no trumps because of the singleton heart, so prefers to continue with spades. If holding an outstanding suit such as ♠AKQ1098 or similar, South would have opened 2♠, so North knows to treat the suit with caution. However, South's bid has struck oil and North has no fears about partner's holding with five card support.

The Three Level

If a one-level opening shows a hand with at least 12 points, and the two-level shows a strong hand with at least eight tricks, what on earth does a three-level opening show? How much stronger can you be?

In fact, just to make things totally confusing, a three-level opening is used to describe *a weak hand with a very long suit*. It is usually referred to as a *'pre-emptive bid'*. What is the thinking behind such a manoeuvre?

The idea in making a pre-emptive bid is a simple one – to prevent the opponents from getting the best out of their cards, whilst taking little risk. In other words, a chance to make a nuisance of yourself!

Here are a few possible pre-emptive openings, see what you think:

(a)	♠ AQ106543	(b)	♠ 7	(c)	♠ K1086543
	♡ A54		♡ KQJ9874		♡ Q4
	◊ 7		◊ Q108		◊ Q4
	♣ 73		♣ 73		♣ J7

(d)	♠ 7	(e)	♠ 7	(f)	♠ J1086
	♡ 72		♡ 65		♡ 7
	◊ 732		◊ QJ1098654		◊ AK109754
	♣ AK109875		♣ K6		♣ 7

Which of these would you open at the three level? This is my view:

(a) Open 1♠. The hand is too strong for a pre-empt, with two aces and a good seven card suit. There is sufficient high-card strength allied to trick-taking potential to warrant opening 1♠.

(b) 3♡. A nice 'solid' heart suit, and the chance to develop a diamond trick make this an ideal candidate for a pre-emptive bid. But remember that, by opening at a high level, you are forcing the opponents to gamble. They often double your contract and take a 'sure plus'. It is essential, therefore, that we do not get carried away with our pre-empts and incur some over-sized penalties.

Aim to have six certain tricks when non-vulnerable or seven tricks if vulnerable. This is often referred to as the '*Rule of 500*', as that will be the penalty if partner produces nothing of value, as you find partners are prone to do.

On that basis, this hand is ideal for 3♡ if non-vulnerable, but doubtful otherwise. Whether you decide to pre-empt on marginal hands is very much a matter of temperament, i.e. how philosophically you can accept the occasional inevitable disaster. In general the more often you pre-empt, the harder you are to play against (and with!).

(c) Pass. Wholly unsuitable for a pre-empt. You have nothing but losers outside spades and your suit is moth-eaten. Without an unsuitable dummy, this hand could produce a four figure penalty, for example:

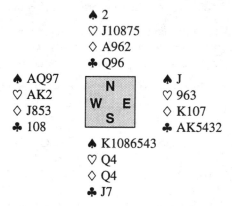

```
                    ♠ 2
                    ♡ J10875
                    ◇ A962
                    ♣ Q96
  ♠ AQ97          N          ♠ J
  ♡ AK2                       ♡ 963
  ◇ J853      W       E       ◇ K107
  ♣ 108           S           ♣ AK5432
                    ♠ K1086543
                    ♡ Q4
                    ◇ Q4
                    ♣ J7
```

South plays in 3♠ doubled and makes ...? With 4 spades, 2 hearts, 1 diamond and 2 clubs to lose, it is in fact East/West who make 3♠! Be warned. I have rarely found partners to be sympathetic in these situations.

(d) 3♣. A good example of a three-level opener, particularly non-vulnerable. Such a hand can be used constructively as you will see shortly.

(e) 3◇. The extra card in diamonds compensates for missing the ace and king.

(f) Pass to begin with and, overcall diamonds later. It is very dangerous to open at the three level on a hand which has potential to play well in another suit. If partner has a moderate hand, he will nearly always pass your opening and you may find you have missed the boat, for example:

(i)	♠ KQ9	(ii)	♠ Q9743	(iii)	♠ AK9543
	♡ J1084		♡ AJ4		♡ 932
	◇ Q8		◇ 6		◇ 62
	♣ A842		♣ AJ82		♣ A6
	(5◇)		(4♠)		(6♠!)

Partner would pass 3◇ on all these hands and yet you can make at least game every time.

Responding to Three-Level Openers

As the primary purpose of a three-level bid is to shut out the opponents, it figures that you will need a good hand to respond to such a bid. Unless you are 'raising the ante', by supporting partner, this is indeed true. There is little point in mentioning a suit of your own, just for the sake of it, when it is highly unlikely that your partner will have any support for you.

Partner has opened 3♣ – how do you deal with these hands?

(a)	♠6	(b)	♠AQ10864	(c)	♠AJ4
	♡A962		♡KJ53		♡KJ7
	◇AK52		◇J7		◇Q1084
	♣J1082		♣5		♣K63

I would suggest the following:

(a) 5♣. Opposite an average pre-empt, there is a reasonable expectation of making 5♣, for example:

♠ 72
♡ 85
◇ 94
♣ AK97654

(b) Pass. These is little point in bidding spades because your suit will not be as good as partner's, or at least it shouldn't be! A 'change of suit' shows a good hand and is 'forcing for one round', i.e. the pre-emptor must make at least one more bid. To respond 3♠, you might have something like:

♠ AKJ1094
♡ AK2
◇ 73
♣ K6

and be investigating the possibilities of 4♠ as an alternative to the 'obvious' 5♣.

(c) 3NT. You have the stops, let's hope partner supplies the tricks. Whilst it is true that 3NT is no certainty, it is nevertheless a reasonable gamble opposite an average pre-empt:

♠ 108
♡ 64
◇ 93
♣ AQJ9875

You have a good chance and the added advantage that the defence feels under pressure when they can see a long suit in dummy. Pressure leads to panic and panic leads to errors.

What happens if partner pre-empts in a major, does that change our outlook? How would you respond with the following hands if partner opened 3♠?

(a) ♠ 7   **(b)** ♠ K32   **(c)** ♠ 7
   ♡ AK103   ♡ Q1042   ♡ KQ108654
   ◇ A765   ◇ KJ9   ◇ A32
   ♣ KQ82   ♣ AQ4   ♣ 75

Here are my suggestions:

(a) 4♠. Don't be tempted into bidding 3NT despite your wealth of stoppers. You do not have enough tricks and your singleton spade will preclude you from enjoying your partner's suit. Just imagine the relative merits of 3NT and 4♠ if you were facing:

♠ KQJ9862
♡ 72
◇ 82
♣ 93

(b) 3NT. This is the ideal hand for a 3NT bid despite, and in fact because of, holding better spade support. There is every chance that 4♠ may lose four tricks, whereas 3NT will make easily, for example:

♠ AQ109765
♡ 65
◊ 85
♣ 93

(c) Pass. Although it is annoying to be pre-empted by partner, it happens from time to time. Bidding because you do not like his suit will only result in this type of sequence:

West	North	East	South
–	3♠	Pass	4♡
Pass	4♠	Pass	5♡
Dble!	5♠	Dble!	Pass
Pass	Pass		

As someone once said to me – 'Too undignified for words'.

Best to pass and leave well alone.

The Four Level

Four-level openings describe similar hands to three-level pre-empts but, as you would no doubt expect, they are about a trick or so stronger. Here are a few examples:

(a)   Open 4 ♣ on   ♠ 8
                                      ♡ –
                                        ◊ J987
                                        ♣ KQ1098765

(b)   Open 4 ◊ on   ♠ 8
                                        ♡ 8
                                        ◊ AQJ10987
                                        ♣ K1097

(c)   Open 4 ♡ on   ♠ 4
                                        ♡ AKQ10987
                                        ◊ Q987
                                        ♣ 6

(d)   Open 4 ♠ on   ♠ QJ1098763
                                ♡ –
                                ◊ KQ82
                                ♣ 7

Because of the wide-range of distributions and point counts, it is important not to go 'slamming' at the drop of a hat. Here are three hands which are facing partner's 4♡ opening; only one should bid a slam. Which one?

(i) ♠ AQJ965   **(ii)** ♠ KQ6   **(iii)** ♠ A43
         ♡ A32   ♡ KJ   ♡ KQ
         ◊ 7   ◊ AQ10432   ◊ A765
         ♣ Q104   ♣ K5   ♣ A1082

The answer (iii), because it has support for any outside suit, *and* can guarantee to shore up trumps. Both the others have weaknesses which make a slam most improbable, for example, (ii) is missing three aces. There is little to be gained by playing for a miracle hand opposite, better to pass and take your plus.

That concludes higher-level openings. I will leave you to decide when you want to open at the five and six level. As a suggestion, my wife and I bid a few practice hands recently, and she dealt herself:

                    ♠ –
                    ♡ KQJ1098765432
                    ◊ A
                    ♣ –

Not that you will get rich worrying about what to do with this hand, but I would advise opening 6♡ and trust your partner to raise to a grand slam with ♡A!

7

RANGE OF 1NT AND 2NT OPENINGS AND REBIDS

We discussed opening 1NT in *Play Bridge at Home* without ever really defining its strength. The reason for that apparent omission is that it is possible to use 1NT to show different ranges. There are no 'rules' governing the exact point count required.

In most parts of the world, a 1NT opening is referred to as 'strong', showing about 15 to 17 points (most 'ranges' are expressed this way). You will find that the defined range is usually narrow (2 or 3 points at most) to assist in constructive bidding. So for a French player, 1NT could describe any of these hands:

(a) ♠ AQ103   (b) ♠ Q98   (c) ♠ 106
    ♡ AJ7   ♡ AJ753   ♡ AQ4
    ◇ K104   ◇ AQ   ◇ KJ7
    ♣ Q98   ♣ KJ4   ♣ AJ985

Despite giving great security from being doubled and conceding large penalties, most social players nevertheless avoid the strong no trump. This is because it is necessary to use some 'prepared' openings to assist in dealing with weaker hands. Again, if you were French you would open all these hands with 1♣:

(i) ♠ KQ107 (ii) ♠ Q10   (iii) ♠ Q1084
   ♡ AJ7   ♡ A43   ♡ A987
   ◇ K104   ◇ Q2   ◇ AQ
   ♣ 432   ♣ AJ10876 ♣ 732

It is hard to improve your bidding judgement, particularly in the early stages of learning, if bids do not relate to the holding in the suit, as with (i) and (iii) above.

In the UK we prefer the slightly riskier, but more natural, *'weak no trump'* i.e. 12-14 points. In effect a minimum bid means a minimum hand. Hence, a British 1NT looks like this:

(a) ♠ Q1084	**(b)** ♠ J984	**(c)** ♠ AQ6
♡ Q108	♡ AQ102	♡ J9852
◇ AJ7	◇ 108	◇ A7
♣ K94	♣ AQ4	♣ Q107

Note that a five-card major is permissible if it is of poor quality *and* you have 'stops' in all the other suits. Because you have dealt with your minimum openings effectively, there is no need to 'prepare' other bids. Thus if you open 1♣, you always have four or more clubs.

How do we deal with stronger balanced hands? The table below should help explain.

Point Count	Action Taken
12-14	Open 1NT
15-16	Open a suit & rebid no trumps at lowest level
17-18	Open a suit & jump one level in no trumps
19-20	Open a suit & jump to 3NT
21-22	Open 2NT
23+	Open 2♣ & rebid no trumps

Quiz

Here is a brief test on the treatment of balanced hands:

How do you propose to express the following?

(a) ♠ AQ104	**(b)** ♠ Q106	**(c)** ♠ Q6543
♡ AJ94	♡ J85	♡ K72
◇ A7	◇ 62	◇ AQ
♣ 652	♣ AKQ94	♣ K93

(d) ♠ AJ92	**(e)** ♠ AKJ107	**(f)** ♠ Q106
♡ K7	♡ AQ6	♡ AKJ94
◇ QJ9	◇ A4	◇ A72
♣ AK108	♣ AJ9	♣ AJ

Answers

(a) Open 1♡ (lower of touching 4-card suits) and rebid as follows:

Over 1♠	Raise to 3♠
Over 1NT	Pass (1NT is usually up to 9 points, so game cannot be a good proposition)
Over 2♣ or 2♢	Bid 2NT
Over 2♡	Pass (as for 1NT)

(b) Open 1♣. Many players would open 1NT, but I prefer to stick to a suit when it expresses my hand so well. Plan to rebid 2♣ over 1♢ or to raise a major suit response. To open 1NT would be sound on:

$$\spadesuit \ Q106$$
$$\heartsuit \ J85$$
$$\diamondsuit \ A6$$
$$\clubsuit \ KQ942$$

A hand with more general strength.

(c) Open 1NT. The alternative action of opening 1♠ and then rebidding the suit (remember you do not have enough points to rebid no trumps) does not accurately describe your hand.

(d) Open 1♠. Always choose a major in preference to a minor with a strong balanced hand (17+ points). This is because a four-four fit is occasionally lost when you rebid no trumps. It rarely matters if a minor suit fit disappears, but could cost points in a major. Plan to rebid as follows:

Over 1NT	Raise to 2NT (3NT if you held 19-20 points)
Over 2♣, 2♢ or 2♡	Bid 3NT
Over 2♠	Bid 2NT

(e) Open 2♣ and rebid 2NT showing 23-24 points. If you are lucky enough to hold an even better hand (say 25-26 points), rebid 3NT.

(f) Open 1♡ and then bid 3NT over all simple responses.

I hope that gives you a flavour of how to handle balanced hands but, before I leave them, two points need to be stressed:

1. Do not be too concerned about the exact shape of the hand. A 4-3-3-3, 4-4-3-2 or 5-3-3-2 is balanced, and should be dealt with as such, even if the five card suit is a major (provided it is of poor quality).

2. High-card points do not tell you everything. Be flexible and be prepared to up-grade or down-grade hands, for example:

(a) ♠ A108	**(b)** ♠ KQ	**(c)** ♠ QJ10
♡ Q109	♡ QJ4	♡ A4
◇ A7	◇ A652	◇ AQJ109
♣ KQJ94	♣ K652	♣ A107

(a) Despite having 16 high-card points (HCPs), the hand is worth nearer to 18, because of its intermediates (10s and 9s) and a good five-card suit.

(b) Instead of 15 HCPs, it is worth less than many 14 point hands. It lacks intermediates, and most of the high cards are in the shorter suits.

(c) With 18 points this hand is worth at least 19 points, for reasons similar to those in (a).

So don't be afraid to bid these hands according to their worth, rather than their exact number of points.

8
JUMP RESPONSES

I could sub-title this chapter 'Jumping for Joy', as it adequately expresses what a jump response in a new suit is all about. It is designed to show your partner that you have at least a good opening bid. Hence *game is guaranteed* and even a slam may be available. After a jump response, neither partner can pass until game has been reached.

Here are a few hands to illustrate jump responses:

Your partner opens 1♢, what do you bid on:

(a) ♠ AJ9   (b) ♠ AK1094   (c) ♠ AJ6
    ♡ 6   ♡ A654   ♡ AKJ9
    ♢ Q1084   ♢ A2   ♢ Q104
    ♣ AKQ106   ♣ Q7   ♣ K65

(d) ♠ AKQJ973 (e) ♠ AK1073
    ♡ 632   ♡ AK1073
    ♢ 65   ♢ 653
    ♣ A   ♣ –

Answers

(a) 3♣. Then follow-up by supporting diamonds with the security of it being a forcing bid. Your partner will know you have a good club suit, sixteen or more points and diamond support. Not a bad description, to be sure.

(b) 2♠. Then 3♡. With a slightly weaker hand, I would advise a 1♠ response, for example:

              ♠ AQ1094
              ♡ A654
              ♢ K2
              ♣ J7

Bid 1♠ and then 3♡. This approach will show an upper limit of about 15 points.

(c) 2♡.   Then follow with no trumps to show the balanced nature of your hand.

(d) 2♠.   Even though you are deficient in high card points, the trick taking potential of this hand thoroughly justifies a jump response or 'force'. Just keep bidding spades and partner will soon get the picture.

(e) 2♠.   Then follow with 3♡. Again, we can 'cheat' a little and force with 14 points, because we have such good suits *and* a fit for partner's diamonds. With:

> ♠ AK1073
> ♡ AK1073
> ◇ –
> ♣ 653

content yourself with 1♠ over 1◇, and follow with 3♡. The hand is not as good with a void in partner's main suit.

Using a jump response is helpful for two reasons:

(i) It immediately establishes that a game is certain and suggests a slam contract may be on.

(ii) It limits any other bidding by responder, so that many fruitless searches for higher level contracts can be avoided. For example:

Dealer South. Love All.

> ♠ AQ1086
> ♡ AJ87
> ◇ Q6
> ♣ 53

> ♠ 53
> ♡ K4
> ◇ AJ8
> ♣ AQ10986

West	North	East	South
–	–	–	1♣
Pass	1♠	Pass	2♣
Pass	3♡	Pass	3NT
Pass	Pass	Pass	

South has no difficulty 'signing off' in 3NT over partner's second round jump to 3♡, even though holding a first-class hand. This is because South knows that North cannot have more than 15 points, so there is just not enough strength between the two hands to justify a shot at a slam. However:

Dealer South. Love All.

♠ AQ1086
♡ AQ97
◊ Q6
♣ K5

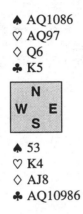

♠ 53
♡ K4
◊ AJ8
♣ AQ10986

West	North	East	South
–	–	–	1♣
Pass	2♠	Pass	3♣
Pass	3♡	Pass	4♣
Pass	5♣	Pass	6♣
Pass	Pass	Pass	

Here South keeps the bidding alive over 3♡ in the high hopes of better things. The reward is to reach a good, if not completely certain, slam.

I have now covered most aspects of 'Constructive bidding', i.e. where you and your partner are the only two active players. In the final book of the series, I will look in detail at 'Competitive Bidding', i.e. both sides are bidding, as well as some conventions and agreements that should help us.

Conclusion

I sincerely hope that you have enjoyed *Improve Your Bridge at Home* and found it stimulating and informative. If you have fully taken on-board all that the first two books contain, you will already have achieved quite a good standard at the game.

In the final book of the series, *Winning Bridge at Home* I will complete your initiation. As the title suggests, I will be building on themes already covered and taking them to an advanced level. Don't be worried by that, you will simply find it an extension of what you have already learnt.

In particular, I will deal with:

Declarer Play
Advanced techniques, end plays, loser-on-loser, ruffing finesses
Psychology
How to handle good and bad contracts

Defence
Falsecards and deception
Advanced signalling
Unblocking, ducking and hold-up plays

Bidding
Competitive bidding
The Natural system
Conventions
Slam bidding
Doubles and re-doubles

Plenty of topics to get through and I hope you will join me to consider them.